A PERFORMER'S GUIDE TO MUSIC

of THE

Classical Period

Series Editor
Anthony Burton

The Associated Board of
the Royal Schools of Music

First published in 2002 by

The Associated Board of the Royal Schools of Music (Publishing) Limited

24 Portland Place, London W1B 1LU, United Kingdom

Reprinted in 2004, 2007, 2009

© 2002 by The Associated Board of the Royal Schools of Music

ISBN 978 1 86096 193 9

AB 2765

A CIP catalogue for this book is available from The British Library.

Design and formatting by Geoffrey Wadsley
Music origination by Jack Thompson
CD compilation and mastering by Ken Blair (BMP Recording)
Printed in England by Halstan & Co. Ltd, Amersham, Bucks

Contents

Illustrations

Notes on the Contributors

Jane Glover studied at St Hugh's College, Oxford, and began her conducting career as an adjunct to her scholarly research, conducting her own editions of seventeenth-century Venetian operas. A former music director of Glyndebourne Touring Opera and artistic director of the London Mozart Players, she is now in demand all over the world as a conductor of operas, orchestral music and major choral works. Among her many recordings are highly praised discs of symphonies and other works by Haydn and Mozart.

David Wyn Jones is reader in music at the University of Wales, Cardiff. He has written and lectured extensively on the music of the Classical period. He was the editor of the Oxford Composer Companion to Haydn, and has written a study of Beethoven's Pastoral Symphony and a short life of Beethoven. He has also edited music of the Classical period, and acted as consultant for the series of recordings of Haydn's masses performed by Collegium Musicum 90 under Richard Hickox.

Cliff Eisen studied at Toronto and Cornell Universities, and taught at New York University, before becoming reader in historical musicology at King's College, London. He specializes in the music of Mozart, as author and editor, as associate editor of the new Köchel catalogue, and as editor of the Oxford Composer Companion to Mozart. He has a particular interest in Classical performing practice, and acted as adviser for the series of recordings of Mozart's piano concertos by Robert Levin with the Academy of Ancient Music and Christopher Hogwood.

David Ward studied at Cambridge University, at the Royal College of Music in London, where his piano teachers included Cyril Smith and Katharina Wolpe, and in Paris with Nadia Boulanger. He has performed as a pianist in many countries, and his special interest in music of the Classical period has led him to take up also the fortepiano, harpsichord and clavichord. He teaches at the Royal College of Music and the Birmingham Conservatoire, lectures on early keyboard instruments for the European Piano Teachers' Association, and is an examiner for the Associated Board.

Duncan Druce has for many years been well known as a performer on violin and viola, in both contemporary music and early music ensembles – the latter including The Music Party, which pioneered period-instrument performance of music of the Classical period. He is also a composer: his output includes orchestral, choral and chamber music, and reconstructions of several incomplete works, notably a highly praised edition of the Mozart Requiem. Formerly senior lecturer in music at Bretton Hall College in West Yorkshire, he now combines part-time university teaching with his performing and composing activities.

Colin Lawson is internationally known for his performances and recordings on period clarinets, as a concerto soloist, in chamber music, and as an orchestral principal. His performing activities have run in parallel with an academic career: having taught at the universities of Aberdeen, Sheffield and London, he was appointed a pro vice-chancellor of Thames Valley University in 2001. He is joint editor of, and a major contributor to, the series of Cambridge Handbooks on historical performance, and has also edited the Cambridge Companions to the Clarinet and to the Orchestra.

Richard Wigmore studied languages at Cambridge University, and singing and piano at the Guildhall School of Music & Drama in London. He has combined a career as a professional singer, specializing in oratorio and lieder, with writing and broadcasting. His collection of translations of all Schubert's lieder was published in 1988, and he is now preparing a study of Haydn's life and music.

Barry Cooper was a lecturer in music at the University of Aberdeen from 1974 until 1990, when he moved to the University of Manchester. He is well known as a musicologist, especially in the field of Beethoven studies; he was general editor of *The Beethoven Compendium*, a standard reference work on the composer. His identification of sketches for Beethoven's unfinished Tenth Symphony, and his preparation of a performing version of its first movement, attracted widespread attention.

Anthony Burton studied music at Cambridge University, and worked as an arts administrator in New England and in Manchester before spending fifteen years as a music producer and manager for BBC Radio 3. He is now a freelance broadcaster and writer, covering a wide range of musical subjects. He was guest artistic director of the 2001 Spitalfields Festival in east London.

Acknowledgements

Acknowledgement for permission to reproduce illustrations and music examples is due to the following:

Illustrations
The Art Archive/Museum der Stadt Wien/Dagli Orti: Fig. 1.1
Ashmolean Museum, Oxford/ The Hill Collection: Fig. 4.2
The Bate Collection of Musical Instruments, University of Oxford: Fig. 5.7
The British Library, London: Figs 4.1, 4.3, 4.4
The Cobbe Collection Trust: Figs 3.2, 3.4, 3.6
By courtesy of Fürst zu Oettingen-Wallerstein: Fig. 5.1
Getty Images, London: Fig. 1.2
International Stiftung Mozarteum, Salzburg: Fig. 3.5
Lebrecht Music Collection, London: Figs 5.2, 5.3, 5.4, 5.5, 5.6 (all photos G. Salter), 6.1, 6.3
© The Board of the Trustees of the Victoria & Albert Museum: Figs 3.1, 6.2

Text quotation and music examples
From *Baroque Music Today: Music as Speech* by Nikolaus Harnoncourt, translated by Mary O'Neill, © 1988, published by Amadeus Press. Reproduced by kind permission: p. 45
© Copyright 1947 in USA by Boosey & Co. Ltd. Copyright for all countries. Reproduced by permission of Boosey & Hawkes Music Publishers Ltd: Ex. 1.1
The British Library, London: Exx. 2.6, 2.16, 2.17b, 7.1, 7.2, 7.4
International Stiftung Mozarteum, Salzburg: Ex. 2.17a
Österreichische Nationalbibliothek, Wien, S. H. Beethoven 134. Reproduced by kind permission: Ex. 7.3
From 'Tempo and Character in Beethoven's Music' by Rudolf Kolisch, *Musical Quarterly* 77 (1993), 268–342. Reproduced by permission of Oxford University Press: Table 2.1

Front and back covers
The Quartet – Dupont, Vachon, Rodolphe, Provers and Vernier by Louis Carrogis Carmontelle (1717–1806): The Bridgeman Art Library, London/ Laauros-Giraudon (Musée Condé, Chantilly, France).

General Notes

Where appropriate, note pitches are described using the Helmholtz system:

In the captions to the music examples, the date refers to composition unless given in brackets, in which case it is the date of publication or, in the case of stage works, first performance.

The symbol ⑩ is a cross-reference to the accompanying CD and the Notes on the CD on pp. 107–10.

Anthony Burton

Preface

What does it mean if you have played or sung a piece, and a friend, or a teacher, or an adjudicator, comments: 'That had a good sense of style'; or maybe 'That wasn't very stylish'? It means that the piece was performed with – or without – an understanding of how the composer would have expected it to sound at the time it was written. And it is to help you to find out what composers would have expected in different periods, and to apply your knowledge to your own playing or singing, that these Performer's Guides have been written.

In fact, until the early twentieth century the idea of 'period style' hardly existed. When music of the seventeenth or eighteenth centuries was revived it was usually treated, by editors and performers, as if it belonged to the present day. But as the century went on, musicians began to realize that they could not safely assume that everything – including instruments, and ways of playing them – had simply been getting better all the time, and so that their usual performing style was bound to suit any piece of music equally well.

They began to look for ways of performing music of the past with greater regard for the composer's expectations: through the revival of instruments like the harpsichord and the lute, and the formation of chamber orchestras; through a growth in 'Urtext' editions, which showed (or claimed to show) nothing but the composer's intentions; through the detailed study of 'performance practice', the way music was interpreted at different times and in different places; and more recently through the widespread use of instruments of the same period as the music (or, more often than not, exact modern copies). In all this, recordings played a major part, opening up many neglected areas of musical history, as well as throwing new light on well-known works by demonstrating how their composers might have expected them to sound.

For a while, these developments led to a dismaying move to leave whole areas of repertoire to the specialists: to frown on any performance of Baroque music on the piano; to remove not just Bach and Handel, but even Haydn and Mozart, from the programmes of symphony orchestras. But this was hardly fair to the performers or to their audiences; and for students wishing to get to know a wide range of music, probably without any chance of access to period instruments, it made no sense at all. In any case, as specialist performers and scholars extended their researches into the more familiar territory of the nineteenth century, they discovered that here too there were performing traditions which have been lost or misunderstood. So it has become increasingly clear that all performances of music of the past can benefit from the knowledge and experience gained by the 'early music movement'.

One area which has lagged behind in this has been education. Very often, only those performers who have got as far as music college or university (and by no means all of those) have been exposed to ideas about period performance. And there have been few books presenting reliable information about the interpretation of the music of the past in a general, non-specialist way.

That is the gap we hope to fill with this series of three guides to the performance of music of different periods: the Baroque period roughly defined as from about 1600 to 1759 (the death of Handel); the Classical from 1759 (Haydn's first symphony) to 1828 (the death of Schubert); the Romantic from 1828 (the composition of Berlioz's Op. 1) to about 1914. The guides are aimed broadly at the Associated Board's own constituency of students (especially at the higher grades) and their teachers – not to mention examiners! But they are not designed as companions to specific exam syllabuses, present or future; and we hope they will be useful to all musicians, including adult amateurs and indeed professionals.

The three volumes all have the same plan. An introductory chapter sketches the historical background to the music of the period; a closing chapter discusses sources and editions. The writers of these, all leading experts in their fields, have taken distinctly different approaches to their tasks, so that the three volumes together offer an introduction to different ways of treating music history and musicology.

In between, each volume has an important general chapter on how the music on the page would have been interpreted by performers at the time, followed by a series of more specialized chapters devoted to keyboard, string and wind instruments and singing. All these are written by musicians who have not only scholarly expertise but also practical experience of performing, often at the highest level. One important point which emerges from these chapters is that different kinds of musicians have always learned from each other. We hope you will read all the chapters, not just those devoted to your own speciality; and also that you will gain enlightenment and stimulation from all the tracks on the accompanying CD.

Another important point which the contributors make many times over is that the task of the performer is not simply to give the most accurate account possible of the notes on the printed page. This is an ideal which has been in circulation only for a very few years in the later twentieth century. In general, for centuries, the performer has been expected to bring his or her own skill and taste to bear on the composer's conception – and in some periods to make a very substantial contribution. So we hope you will treat these guides not as a set of instructions telling you how to achieve a 'correct' interpretation, but as a source of the information you will need in order to give a stylish performance – a collaboration between the composer's inspiration in the past and your own imagination and fantasy in the present.

Jane Glover

Introduction

The most arresting description of the period covered in this admirable book, including as it does the years of the French Revolution and the ensuing social and political complexity, comes from Charles Dickens. His *A Tale of Two Cities* opens with a celebrated, spectacular fanfare:

> It was the best of times, it was the worst of times, it was the age of wisdom, it was the age of foolishness, it was the epoch of belief, it was the epoch of incredulity, it was the season of Light, it was the season of Darkness, it was the spring of hope, it was the winter of despair, we had everything before us, we had nothing before us, we were all going direct to Heaven, we were all going direct the other way.

And yet it is arguable that the most remarkable feature of the music written between 1759 and 1828 was stability. Much of the eccentric evolution of the previous century was gradually standardized in an Age of Enlightenment which stood for elegance, symmetry, proportion, simplicity even. And, before the violence erupted again in the rich chaos of nineteenth-century Romanticism, the steadying procedures yielded long-term benefit.

First, the establishment of new musical forms (especially, of course, the ubiquitous 'sonata form'), and the regimen therefore of related harmonic procedure, laid foundations that would far outlast the aesthetic of the age. Secondly, the continued development in the construction of instruments – from newcomers like the pianoforte and the clarinet to new designs for string instruments – and the sounds they produced, both separately and together, gave greater coherence and identity to specific musical genres. And the combination of these two developments led to the formation and standardization of larger orchestras – from that consisting of strings, oboes and horns (as in early Haydn) to the Classical set-up of Beethoven and Schubert (strings, double winds and brass), towards the eclectic gatherings assembled by the brilliant curiosity of Berlioz.

There were developments, too, in music notation. As Cliff Eisen's article here explains, composers were finding more devices and symbols with which to instruct their interpreters. But music notation is always ultimately inadequate. Inconsistencies, conflicts, and, worst of all, gaps in information can still be utterly baffling to any performer. And it is here that the learned experience pervading the articles in this volume will be of great value.

The performance of any piece of music should always be approached from what precedes it, rather than from what follows it. Thus, a Handel aria should be guided by the stylistic implications of Purcell, not Mozart;

and a Mozart sonata untrammelled by Beethoven. For all the vast developments of music in this period, therefore, I have always found it essential to remember that the two areas of music which shaped the output of the Baroque era were dance and solo singing; and that these continued to underlie music of the Classical era, even in genres – like the solo sonata or the string quartet – which seem far removed from them. Minuets, gavottes, gigues, sarabandes, sicilianas, even marches are never far from the surface; and an awareness of this in shaping and phrasing can bring all music alive in a vibrant way. Similarly, the performance of any Classical melody, on any instrument, is often enhanced and aerated by imagining it sung, and breathing and shaping accordingly. The seamless outpouring of long horizontal lines is still a long way off.

The revival of interest in original instruments in recent years has provided much insight into how we should now be performing music of this period; and here the performer will be greatly informed by the articles by Colin Lawson and Duncan Druce. Even with modern instruments, the lessons that we have learnt can be applied. The sound of a modern chamber orchestra, for example, can be transformed by using 'Baroque' timpani with wooden sticks, or natural trumpets and horns, or wooden flutes; and also by a whole range of string techniques, mostly concerning the bow speed and articulation, and the use or not of vibrato. And of course such things can be applied too in solo performance.

Like its companions in the series, this book will be invaluable to performers of all ages and standards, and also to their teachers. It will help the player to make decisions not based on the self-perpetuating mimesis of the recording industry, but made in a context of historically informed awareness. But ultimately one must always let instinct ride information: be obedient to symbols and instructions, but not confined by them. Use this marvellous compendium of information to liberate your response to the music; and enjoy it.

David Wyn Jones

Historical Background

Why 'classical'?

The word 'classical' is used in two accepted senses when talking or writing about music: 'classical' meaning art music, as opposed to pop music or folk music; and, more specialized, Classical denoting the period in the history of Western art music from *c*.1750 to *c*.1830. In the latter sense it is often coupled with the word 'Viennese' in recognition of the fact that all four of the commanding figures of the period, Joseph Haydn (1732–1809), Wolfgang Amadeus Mozart (1756–91), Ludwig van Beethoven (1770–1827) and Franz Schubert (1797–1828), were associated with the city of Vienna. But none of these composers would have been familiar with the idea of a 'classical' composer, in either sense. The terms 'Viennese Classical school', 'Classical period' and 'Viennese classics' came into common use only at the end of the nineteenth century and the beginning of the twentieth, when commentators surveying the development of music saw the style of Haydn, Mozart, Beethoven and Schubert as the foundation of the music of their own times. In that sense the four were honoured and revered, or 'classical' in that they were special and old. Gradually the term 'Classical period' gained a secondary meaning that helped to establish its currency: if 'classical' could also imply restraint, poise and elegance, then it was a useful label to separate composers such as Haydn, Mozart, Beethoven and Schubert from the 'Romantic' composers, who were more inclined to be expressive, wayward and indulgent.

Like all convenient labels, 'Classical period' has its problems. But those people who first promoted its use a hundred years ago did so in recognition of a simple, indisputable fact: the period *c*.1750 to *c*.1830 saw the formulation of many features of musical style and musical life that were to be central for the next hundred years or so. Indeed, even at the beginning of the twenty-first century musical composition and musical life are heavily influenced by the Classical era.

The period saw the invention of several genres that are still with us today: the solo sonata, string quartet, piano trio and symphony, among others. These new genres were all instrumental, which indicates a more general change: instrumental music was increasingly given the same status as vocal music. The most international genre in the later Baroque period was Italian opera; by the end of the Classical period the most international genre was the symphony. The development of the symphony promoted the appearance of a more standardized orchestra and of public concerts, features which can be traced back in time but which became widespread only during the Classical era. As in the Baroque period, the music that was played was mostly contemporary, but the Classical period also witnessed an increasing interest in performing older music alongside new and recent works. This trend gained momentum during the Romantic period, until it reached the point where most performances were of old rather than new works: music had become part of the so-called museum culture – a situation that it is difficult to imagine will ever change.

Although instrumental music gained in importance in the Classical period, vocal music continued to thrive, with some notable new developments. In opera, composers such as Christoph Willibald Gluck (1714–87) and Mozart sought increasing dramatic realism in their works, whether the subject matter was serious or comic; indeed, while the old-fashioned *opera seria* died out in the later eighteenth century, Mozart's operatic comedies offered an equally serious and more detailed treatment of human nature and relationships. The dominance of the Italian language was challenged as composers of operas in French or German, in particular, began to claim artistic parity. Beethoven's only opera, *Fidelio*, is in the form of the German *Singspiel*, which, with its spoken dialogue instead of *secco* (keyboard-accompanied) recitative, had previously been considered a light form. Church music for the Protestant and Catholic liturgies continued to be composed in substantial quantities by composers great and small; though here, too, there was an interesting development: works originally intended for specific church services received concert performances, alongside concertos and symphonies. In this way important works such as Mozart's Requiem, Haydn's *Stabat mater* and Beethoven's Mass in C became part of the concert, as well as the liturgical, repertoire.

One unfortunate legacy of the term 'Viennese Classical school' is that it focuses attention on the great composers who were associated with Vienna, sidelining the dozens or hundreds of composers in the rest of Europe who also contributed to the vitality of musical life. For instance, a music-lover living in London in the second half of the eighteenth century would certainly have been enthusiastic about the music of Haydn, but he or she would probably also have enjoyed the music of other composers: among them Johann Christian Bach (1735–82, the youngest son of J. S. Bach), who lived for over twenty years in the city and who was well known for his symphonies, concertos and operas; the Italian Niccolò Piccinni (1728–1800), composer of the opera *La buona figliuola* (based on Samuel Richardson's novel *Pamela*, and one of the most frequently performed operas of the day throughout Europe); and the Bohemian Adalbert Gyrowetz (1763–1850), who wrote many attractive symphonies.

The verdict of history has been that Haydn, Mozart, Beethoven and Schubert were more challenging and indeed greater composers than the likes of J. C. Bach, Piccinni and Gyrowetz. But all the same, there is a good deal of interesting and entertaining music from this period by so-called minor composers. For instance, another son of J. S. Bach, Carl Philipp Emanuel Bach (1714–88), who worked in Berlin and Hamburg, was one of a number of composers in northern Germany who were dissatisfied with the lightweight emotional content of much music from the middle of the century, in the so-called 'galant' style. There is a more questing, occasionally even eccentric quality in his music, which came to be known as

Fig. 1.1. Haydn at a performance of *The Creation* staged in honour of his seventy-sixth birthday, in the Great Hall of Vienna University on 27 March 1808. From a watercolour by Balthasar Wigand.

'empfindsamer Stil' (literally 'expressive style'). Haydn, Mozart and Beethoven all knew and admired C. P. E. Bach's music. While the main sources of the basic Classical style lay elsewhere – in the poise and balance of the *galant* manner, in the busy forward movement of Italian comic opera, in the finesse of the famous Mannheim court orchestra in southern Germany – the north German 'expressive style' was one of the main sources of inspiration for the profundity and drama in the works of these major figures.

One of the most welcome features of CD recordings of recent years is the increasing number of discs devoted to the lesser figures of the Classical period. They usefully remind us of the broad context in which the great composers worked.

Style and form

Important though the invention of new genres was in the Classical period, it was merely the manifestation of a fundamental and thorough revolution in musical style itself. While the characteristics of the Classical style are quite different from those of the Baroque, they continued to form the basis of the music of the Romantic period: successive generations of composers found a flexibility within the style that encouraged new developments. The Countess's aria 'Porgi amor' (Ex. 1.1, overleaf), from the beginning of Act II of Mozart's opera *Le nozze di Figaro* (The Marriage of Figaro), reveals many features of the Classical style, and, more fascinatingly, how a composer of the first rank was able to find expressive individuality.

The Countess is alone in her boudoir. The audience is already familiar with the philandering ways of her husband, Count Almaviva, and in this aria she laments the loss of his affection. After an orchestral introduction anticipating the singer's melody, the soloist enters at bar 18. The texture of the music has a distinct feeling of foreground and background: the voice, which carries the melody, is supported by a subordinate orchestral

Ex. 1.1. (opposite and below) W. A. Mozart, *Le nozze di Figaro* (1786): Act II, scene i, 'Porgi amor'.

accompaniment (reduced for keyboard in Ex. 1.1). Although the phrase structure here is governed by the patterns of the Italian text, the sense of two balanced phrases, each four bars long (bars 18–21 followed by bars 22–5) is fundamental to the Classical style. (Sometimes symmetry is built out of shorter, two-bar units.) Each four-bar phrase ends with a cadence: perfect into bar 21 and imperfect into bar 25. Also characteristic of the style is the harmonic vocabulary (indicated in roman numerals). Of the six chords used in these eight bars, tonic and dominant are the most common; the simplicity of the basic language and the primacy given to I and V as points of reference are highly distinctive.

Another important feature of the Classical style, often little considered by performers but crucial to the ebb and flow of this music, is the rate of change of harmony, usually called harmonic rhythm to distinguish it from the surface rhythms (the crotchets, quavers, etc. of the music). Typically, the harmonic rhythm of the Classical period is much slower than in Baroque music, and is more varied. Thus in Ex. 1.1 the first vocal phrase consists of one bar of tonic, followed by two bars of dominant, and then one bar of tonic to end. In the second vocal phrase, as well as the harmony itself being more varied, the harmonic rhythm quickens to two chords per bar in bars 22–3 and three in bar 24 – an increase in the rate of change which was a standard way of shaping music during the Classical period, and which has the distinctive effect of drawing the listener into the music.

Any skilful composer in the second half of the eighteenth century – from St Petersburg to London, Stockholm to Rome – could have written these eight bars using the essential building blocks of the Classical style; but, whereas most would have continued broadly in the same manner (clear four-bar phrases, theme and accompaniment, and uncomplicated harmony), a first-rate composer such as Mozart takes this as a starting point for something much more distinctive and eloquent.

The passage from bars 36 to 45 is particularly striking, not least in its use of dynamics: dynamic variety is obviously not something that was invented in the Classical period, but Classical composers are much more liberal and detailed in their markings than their predecessors. The level of the music from when the voice enters to bar 34 had been a constant *piano*, but to suggest the welling of emotion that culminates in the pause on a dominant 7th in bar 36, Mozart indicates a crescendo up to a *forte*. After the pause the music reverts immediately to *piano*, there is an unprecedentedly quick harmonic rhythm of one chord per semiquaver, and all levels of the texture move together with little or no sense of foreground and background. When the music reaches the crucial word 'sospir' (sigh), the harmonic rhythm slows right down to one chord per bar so that the very unusual chord at bar 38 – a dominant minor 9th – can be savoured. To make this even more effective, Mozart brings in a single bassoon precisely at this point, a perfect example of one aspect of the Classical style drawing attention to another. The music moves as if to make a full cadence into bar 40, but instead of an E flat chord, Mozart – in the equivalent of a dash in a sentence – provides an interrupted cadence on to chord vi, giving the music a sense of expansion. Another approach to a full cadence is made at bars 42–3, but again it is thwarted by an interrupted cadence (V–vi), this time intensified by the bass line rising chromatically from B♭ to C, all to draw attention to the word 'morir' (die). Only in bar 45 does the music reach its appointed full cadence.

This deferring of the musical equivalent of a full stop has an interesting effect on our perception of the phrase patterns. An unfeeling mathematician would point out that from the second quaver beat of bar 36 to the first beat of bar 40 is a four-bar phrase; but the syntax of these bars makes the pattern less obvious than before. Rather than the clear subdivisions of 2+2 that characterize the opening vocal line, there is now the more intricate 1+1+2, and even that analysis does damage to the sense of continuity that there is from bar 38 to bar 39. The following bars are yet more uneven in their subdivision: three bars to the interrupted cadence in bar 43, followed by two bars to the perfect cadence. After this passage of highly sophisticated musical vocabulary, grammar and syntax, the aria returns to the norms of musical expression, as heard in the singer's first phrases.

Being alive to the nuances of the Classical style, whether at the service of a text or in instrumental music, is only one of the demands placed on the performer. Another is the need to keep a sure sense of the overall shape and drama of a movement. The Classical period saw the development of one of the most important formal structures in the history of music, 'sonata form'. This is a misleading term in that it suggests that it is found only in works called 'sonata'. It is much more widespread than that, found in all instrumental music and often in vocal music too. Although it is most commonly encountered in opening fast movements of sonatas, concertos, trios, quartets and symphonies, its principles can frequently be found as well in minuets, scherzos, slow movements and final movements. It became so fundamental to the way that composers thought about music that it is worth outlining these principles – though it should be remembered that, in the same way that Mozart manipulates standard musical language in 'Porgi amor', a good composer will find endless possibilities within sonata form.

Sonata form consists of three sections in the psychologically reassuring sequence of presenting musical material, exploring it, and repeating it; these sections are called the 'exposition', 'development' and 'recapitulation'. In the first movement of Beethoven's Piano Sonata in C major Op. 2 No. 3, for instance, these three sections occupy bars 1–90 (in our recording, to 02.33), bars 91–138 (to 03.59) and bars 139–257. The exposition is often marked to be repeated, as in this sonata, though there are plenty of exceptions to this practice. (The repeat has been omitted from our version of the recording.) Occasionally, the development and recapitulation together are to be repeated as well.

Within the exposition there are two main areas: the 'first subject' in the tonic (bars 1–13; to 0.22) and the 'second subject' in the dominant (bars 47–90; 01.19–02.33); this polarization of tonic and dominant keys as architectural pillars reproduces on a large scale the dependence of the harmonic language on chords I and V. The distinction in character found in this sonata between a motivic first subject and a more lyrical second subject is very typical of Beethoven (the first movement of the Fifth Symphony is a familiar example), though it is not by any means the norm:

Haydn, for instance, often minimizes the difference between first and second subjects to the point where it becomes meaningless to use the label 'second subject'. Mozart and Schubert, for their part, are often more generous in providing melodic material, with more than one theme in the tonic and, more commonly, several in the dominant.

The development section is less stable in its course, modulating freely and reworking material presented in the exposition. In the Beethoven sonata, the paragraph of music beginning at bar 129 (03.41) sits on a held dominant note in the bass, channelling the music towards the recapitulation, which arrives at bar 139 (03.59). The recapitulation presents the material in the same order as in the exposition, but with the crucial difference that it remains in the tonic rather than modulating to the dominant: the second subject is heard in C major at bar 181 (05.10). Composers will often avoid duplicating the exact course of the exposition in the recapitulation, striking a balance between satisfying the desire for repetition and providing the occasional subtle, or not so subtle, change. Beethoven is especially fond of adding an extra section at the end, a 'coda' (literally a 'tail') which gives renewed drama to the movement: in this sonata, it begins at bar 218 (06.14).

The market for music

The music of C. P. E. Bach, Beethoven, Haydn, Mozart, Schubert and countless others was aimed at the full range of performers, from amateurs to professionals. Consequently it was performed in a variety of venues, from private drawing-rooms and salons to churches, public halls and opera houses. To a certain extent, individual genres were associated with particular kinds of venue, though many of these associations were not the ones that are familiar to us today.

The traditional market for the keyboard sonata, as well as sonatas for solo instrument and keyboard and the piano trio, was that of the amateur music-maker. Indeed most keyboard sonatas were written for teaching purposes. Towards the end of the eighteenth century, however, the composers of these genres began to make technical demands that could be met only by fully trained performers. Beethoven's piano sonatas show this divided outlook very clearly. Op. 2 No. 3 and its two companions, published in Vienna in 1796, were designed to promote Beethoven's own career as a pianist and teacher in Vienna, rather than being aimed at the traditional amateur market: that is why they were dedicated to Europe's leading composer, Joseph Haydn, rather than to an aristocratic patron who was also a pupil. On the other hand, the Sonata in G major Op. 79, even though it was composed thirteen years later, is a much less ambitious work, and was clearly intended as material for teaching; with this market in mind, it was first published by Muzio Clementi in London.

String quartets (and other ensemble works such as string quintets, piano quartets, sextets, etc.) were from the beginning almost always played by professional musicians, but often for their own pleasure; listeners tended to be privileged eavesdroppers rather than an audience as such. Although quartets were often played in public in concert halls in Paris and London, most of the quartets by Haydn, Mozart, Beethoven and Schubert were not

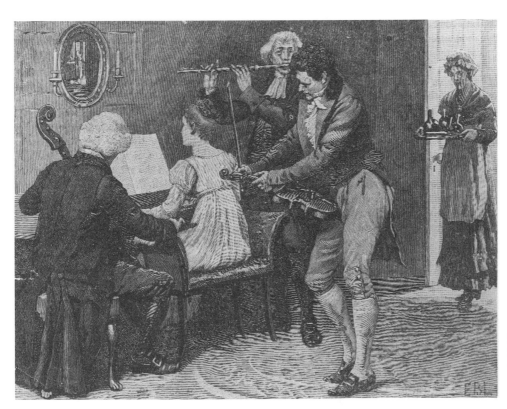

Fig. 1.2. Domestic music-making in the time of King George III (1760–1820). Artist and date unknown.

intended for public performance; as a result all four composers wrote some of their most challenging music for this medium.

While today the concerto and the symphony are the two genres which dominate public concerts, the situation in the Classical period was not so straightforward. Public concert life in some cities, such as Paris, London and Leipzig, did feature performances of concertos and symphonies with orchestras of fifty to sixty players; but Vienna, the supposed capital of music, did not have a fully developed public concert life until well into the nineteenth century. Concertos and symphonies by Haydn, Mozart and Schubert, in particular, were often performed privately rather than publicly, and with much smaller forces than would be found in public performances. For instance, the symphonies Haydn wrote as part of his duties as Kapellmeister (director of music) at the court of Prince Esterházy were played by an orchestra of about fifteen players, and Mozart's piano concertos were sometimes played with one player per part, effectively becoming piano quintets. One further indication that performances could be small-scale was the use of the term 'chamber music' to mean all instrumental music – including concertos and symphonies – that was played in the chamber or room, as opposed to the church or theatre.

While many royal and aristocratic palaces throughout Europe had their own private theatres for performances of operas and plays, most operas in the Classical period were composed for public opera houses with paying audiences (though few theatres held more than 1500 spectators). Except for the crucial fact that all the repertoire was contemporary music, the opera world in the Classical period was little different from that of today:

highly paid singers travelled from one venue to the next, idealized by the public and despaired of by composers and librettists; managers were likely to be as incompetent as they were ambitious. This lethal combination meant that there was hardly a theatre in Europe that did not suffer regular financial crises followed by new beginnings. Mozart struggled valiantly with Viennese opera-house politics in the 1780s to produce his major operas; Beethoven, who, it is sometimes forgotten, was equally keen to compose opera, managed no more than one.

Church music was divided between music composed for the Catholic liturgy and music for the Protestant liturgy, and works were consequently restricted to countries or regions in which the religion for which they were written was officially approved, rather than enjoying the international circulation of operatic and instrumental music. As part of its function within a tradition that was several centuries old, church music tended to be more conservative, following contemporary trends in opera and instrumental music rather than being at the cutting edge of development. In Catholic Austria sacred music was without doubt the most familiar kind of music, since more people, and from a wider social spectrum, attended church than were able to go to concerts or the opera. In cathedrals and larger churches the congregation could expect a rich musical experience. The six standard movements of the mass – Kyrie, Gloria, Credo, Sanctus, Benedictus and Agnus Dei – constituted only the main portion of a communion service, supplemented by Gregorian chant, improvisations on the organ, fanfares played by trumpets and timpani, shorter choral and orchestral works such as Mozart's *Ave, verum corpus*, and instrumental movements from concertos and symphonies. More than one commentator was taken aback by this musical ostentation, and remarked that going to church was more like going to a concert.

What is Classical music about?

In a vocal work such as 'Porgi amor' the function of the music was to reveal the meaning – apparent, implied or hidden – of the text. But what about music without text, such as the many sonatas, trios, quartets, concertos and symphonies that were challenging the traditional primacy of vocal music? Prompted by the popularity of these new genres, many commentators during the Classical period posed this troubling question, without ever being able to give a comprehensive answer. A small minority of instrumental works have titles given to them by the composer to indicate their subject matter: Beethoven's Pastoral Symphony, for instance, evokes the timeless mood of the pastoral, that escapist world of threatened tranquillity, and captures the listener's imagination with orchestral evocations of a brook, birdsong, dancing, a storm and a shepherd's song. Most instrumental music, however, did not have a stated subject matter. Obviously the meaning of such music will be endlessly debated by music theorists, aestheticians, philosophers and psychologists; and, equally obviously, responses will vary from individual to individual, from place to place, and from one era to the next. What musicians in the Classical period considered their music to be about has been much debated in recent years, and offers a great deal of food for thought for modern performers.

Some of the most sophisticated instrumental music of the Classical period has a strong sense of probing and testing the style itself – it is, as it were, music about music. When Haydn said that his 'music was understood all over the world' he was not merely pointing out that his works were very popular; rather he was suggesting that the language in which they were written was used throughout the musical world. For perhaps the first and only time in the history of music, composers throughout Europe shared a musical style with few regional differences, so a highly creative individual such as Haydn could test this shared experience of a musical language, alternately fulfilling expectations and denying them – whether in the way a harmonic progression is used, the disruption of the expected phrase patterns of a minuet, or the distortion of the broader patterns of sonata form. Haydn's task was easier than it would be today, simply because his language was the pervasive one; he did not have to make an impact alongside the very different styles of, say, Monteverdi, J. S. Bach, Verdi, Schoenberg and Birtwistle, to name only five composers. Recapturing this sense of working within a universal language is a real and endlessly fascinating challenge for the modern performer.

When musicians of the Classical period compared music to other art forms, it was hardly ever to painting or architecture, but usually to oratory or spoken drama. This suggests that instrumental music, as well as music with a text, possessed a strong sense of narrative: not in the sense that it tells a story (though sometimes it did) but in the sense of unfolding from one phrase to the next, with care being taken to enunciate the musical 'text' clearly, whether it be declamatory or confidential, complex or simple. When the poet Goethe said that hearing a good string quartet was like 'listening to a stimulating conversation between four intelligent people', he was not being fanciful; rather he was reflecting a commonly held view about music in general. Modern conductors are fond of exhorting players to 'sing'; in music of the Classical period, 'speak to me' might be a more appropriate instruction.

Musicians of the Classical period often thought about the content of a single passage, movement or even piece in terms of it being representative of a more general type of music. Thinking in musical 'topics', as they were called, can be obvious – as when a composer writes a minuet as a movement in a sonata, quartet or symphony – or it can be allusive. In Mozart's *Le nozze di Figaro*, for example, Figaro sings his aria 'Se vuol ballare' (If you want to dance) using the metre, tempo, phrase patterns and rhythms of a minuet, even though the word 'minuet' is never mentioned in the text. References to the rhythms and patterns of the minuet, ländler, contredanse, gavotte, sarabande and other dances, whether conscious or subliminal, permeate the music of all composers from the period. Invoking the world of opera in instrumental music is also a common 'topic', as for instance in the slow movement of Mozart's Piano Concerto K. 271, with its use of recitative-like cadences, or the finale of Beethoven's Fifth Symphony, which 'brings down the curtain' on the preceding drama. Other frequently encountered topics include the hunt, with fast movements in 6/8 time; the learned, that is 'difficult' contrapuntal music in an otherwise chordal context; the virtuoso, as in several passages in the first movement of

Beethoven's Op. 2 No. 3; and the sublime – a climactic sense of being overwhelmed by the beauty, majesty or power of the music, as when Haydn depicts the invention of light near the beginning of his oratorio *The Creation*. Occasionally, one topic will govern a complete movement, providing no contrast of mood, as in 'Porgi amor'; more typical of the Classical style, however, is to offer several topics – some obvious, some perhaps less so – to provide conflict and drama, as in the opening movement of Beethoven's Op. 2 No. 3.

None of the approaches to Classical music discussed here provides by itself a complete explanation of a given piece of music, and identifying a single thought process at work in a piece is as limiting as noting 'where the second subject is'. Music of the Classical period is endlessly complex in its resonances, and all performers can hope to do is to make themselves open to as many of these resonances as possible.

Cliff Eisen

Notation and Interpretation

What do the notes mean?

As a rule, musicians of the last several generations have been trained to assume that performance symbols have a universal meaning, observed by composers throughout history. Nothing could be further from the truth: changes in musical style and aesthetics, in theoretical outlook, and in the construction and capabilities of musical instruments all militate against the idea that there was a common performing practice – and consequently a uniform way to interpret notation – between 1759 and 1828. Eighteenth-century theorists, for example, saw music as based essentially on harmony. In 1806, however, about the mid-point of Beethoven's career and the beginning of Schubert's, Jérôme-Joseph de Momigny (in his *Cours complet d'harmonie et de composition*) argued that a 'horizontal' approach to music should be restored after having been subordinated to a 'vertical' approach.

Differences in descriptions of specific performing practices can also be found. In 1789, for example, Daniel Gottlob Türk (in his piano method *Clavierschule*) recommended that 'when notes are to be played in the usual manner, that is to say, neither staccato nor legato, the finger should be raised from the key a little earlier than the value of the note requires'; in 1801, however, Muzio Clementi wrote that 'The best general rule is to keep down the keys of the instrument, the FULL LENGTH of every note'. And, finally, it was sometimes the case that particular instruments, or particular ways of playing them, were not available on the pan-European stage – or even within regions that we now consider to have been culturally close. When Mozart wanted a specific trumpet and horn sound in *Idomeneo*, he wrote to his father requesting a special kind of mute that was unavailable in Munich but used by the watchmen in Salzburg. Even between these two geographically and culturally close cities, then, there were different musical traditions. How much difference might there have been between Vienna and Berlin and Paris and London?

Accordingly, written sources describing late eighteenth- and early nineteenth-century performing practices must be treated with caution: with what repertoire are they contemporary, and to which works do they really apply? In some cases the answers are unproblematic: C. P. E. Bach's *Versuch über die wahre Art das Clavier zu spielen* (1753, translated as *Essay on the True Art of Playing Keyboard Instruments*), Quantz's *Versuch einer Anweisung die Flöte traversiere zu spielen* (1752, translated as *On Playing the Flute*), and Leopold Mozart's *Versuch einer gründlichen Violinschule* (1756, translated as *A Treatise on the Fundamental Principles of Violin Playing*) can all be associated with specific repertoires. What is more, all three books were highly regarded throughout Europe for much of the eighteenth century – clearly they had something to say to performers everywhere. At the same time, however, it is by no means clear that *all* of what these authors wrote was applicable in every circumstance. Nevertheless, their treatises are well worth studying, as are treatises by students and intimates of well-known performers. These include E. W. Wolf's *Musikalischer Unterricht* (Musical Instruction, 1788), Carl Czerny's *Schule der praktischen Tonsetzkunst* Op. 600 (?1849–50, translated as *School of Practical Composition*), and Johann Nepomuk Hummel's *Ausführlich theoretisch-practische Anweisung zum Piano-forte Spiel* (1828, translated as *A Complete Theoretical and Practical Course of Instructions on the Art of Playing the Piano-Forte*).

Musical sources tell another story, and the information to be derived from them depends in no small part on how their essential nature is perceived. One school of thought – born in the nineteenth century and dying a hard death even today – advocates that only a composer's score, and not a performance, represents the 'substance' of a work: it is as if Mozart with extraordinary ease, and Beethoven with titanic struggle, plucked note-perfect, finished pieces from the ether, not a detail of which can be changed in performance. It is this attitude that encourages performers to claim that they 'let the music speak for itself'. Yet this flies in the face of two very obvious facts: that music *cannot* speak for itself; and that Mozart and Beethoven, and to a lesser extent Haydn and Schubert, were in the first instance performers. Surely they were performer-composers as well, and the extraordinary difficulty of their music, both technically and conceptually, is itself a performance of sorts. A more fruitful approach, then, is to view sources as performances themselves: this is obviously the case with Mozart's autographs, the different chronological layers of which often preserve a number of equally viable readings. Viewed as performances, musical sources open a window on an enormous variety of interpretations.

Perhaps the overwhelming impression one gets from a careful study of works by Haydn, Mozart, Beethoven, Schubert, or any other great composer of the late eighteenth or early nineteenth centuries, is that no single detail seems to be completely independent of its surroundings, whether a single phrase or an entire movement. In what follows, then, the pigeon-holing of notational conventions and interpretation – including tempo and metre, articulation and phrasing, dynamics and ornamentation – is arbitrary at best. There are clues, however, as to ways these discrete topics interact with each other. And there is at least one example that tries to draw together several of the issues discussed here.

Tempo and metre

Tempo is a problematic – and crucial – issue. Jean-Jacques Rousseau, in his *Dictionnaire de musique* (1768), lists three factors that play a part in determining tempo:

> The degree of slowness or quickness that one gives to a measure depends on several things. 1) On the value of the notes that compose the bar. Indeed, one sees that a bar that contains a breve must be taken

more calmly and last longer than that which contains only a crotchet.
2) On the tempo indicated by the French or Italian word that one
ordinarily finds at the head of the piece… Each of these words
indicates an explicit modification in the tempo of a given metre.
3) Finally, on the character of the piece itself, which, if it is well made,
will necessarily make its true tempo felt.

The first of these points refers to the performance practice known as 'fixed tactus': other things being equal, time signatures with smaller denominators move more quickly than those with larger ones (for example, 3/8 is faster than 3/4), and 'short' metres are faster than 'long' metres (for example, 3/8 is a short metre, 6/8 a long metre). Whether this still applied to later eighteenth-century music, however, is uncertain, although E. W. Wolf suggested in 1788 that there are fixed relations among tempo indicators; it is apparently contradicted by passages in which composers rewrite slow introductions but in tempo, typically at recapitulations (there is a good example in the first movement of Mozart's 'Posthorn' Serenade K. 320).

Rousseau's second point, of course, describes terms such as *presto*, *allegro*, *andante*, *adagio* and the like. Yet these, too, are subject to considerable debate, even the ubiquitous common-time *allegro*: while many writers over the period 1750 to 1800 apparently put this at ♩ = 120, others describe speeds ranging from ♩ = 75 to ♩ = 94. Under any circumstances, however, it is important to note that on the whole eighteenth-century tempos were on the fast side in general (though not necessarily as fast as some modern-day 'historically informed' conductors would have us believe). *Andante*, in particular, was a 'walking' tempo that imparts life and movement to so-called 'slow' movements – think, for example, of the Andante con moto of Beethoven's Fifth Symphony. *Andantino*, on the other hand, is problematic, sometimes described as slower than *andante*, sometimes faster. For Mozart, at least, *andantino* was probably a slower tempo: there are instances in his music where the sequence of speeds can only be understood as a linear progression, with *andantino* on the slower side. For other composers, and in other locales, however, the situation may have been different: in 1813 Beethoven wrote to the Scottish publisher George Thomson asking whether he understood *andantino* to be faster or slower than *andante*. The minuet, finally, was also a faster movement, though it is important to recognize two distinctly different types of the dance: one, written with crotchets and quavers, was faster; the other, described by Mozart in 1770 in a letter from Italy as having 'plenty of notes', was more moderate. These two types can be distinguished right up to the early years of the nineteenth century.

Metronomes did not become common until the early nineteenth century, from which time composers, performers and theorists wrote down with increasing frequency not only their ideas about tempos in general but also their requirements for specific works old and new. Beethoven, for example, left metronome markings for all nine of his symphonies, the first eleven string quartets and several smaller works. Among his piano works, however, he left markings only for the 'Hammerklavier' Sonata Op. 106 – and these are controversial, for they seem unreasonably fast. Table 2.1

Table 2.1.
Authentic
metronome marks
for selected works by
Beethoven.

gives a representative sampling. The chief point to emerge from this summary is not only that eighteenth- and early nineteenth-century tempos were faster but that there was no standardization. Hence, neither chronological nor geographical conclusions can be drawn from this overview.

Opus	Work	Movements: Metronome marks
18/5	String Quartet in A major	Allegro ♩. = 104; Menuetto ♩. = 76; Andante cantabile ♪ = 100, Poco adagio ♪ = 88; Allegro o = 76
18/6	String Quartet in B flat major	Allegro con brio o = 80; Adagio ma non troppo ♫ = 80; Scherzo: Allegro ♩. = 63; La Malinconia: Adagio ♪ = 58, Allegretto quasi Allegro ♩. = 88, Poco adagio ♪ = 69, Prestissimo ♩. = 112
20	Septet in E flat major	Adagio ♪ = 72, Allegro con brio ♩ = 96; Adagio cantabile ♪ = 132; Tempo di Minuetto ♩ = 120; Andante ♪ = 120; Scherzo: Allegro molto e vivace ♩. = 126; Andante con moto Marcia ♪ = 76, Presto ♩ = 112
55	Symphony No. 3 ('Eroica')	Allegro con brio ♩. = 60; Marcia funebre: Adagio assai ♪ = 80; Scherzo: Allegro vivace ♩. = 116; Finale: Allegro molto ♩ = 76, Poco andante ♪ = 108, Presto ♩ = 116
59/1	String Quartet in F major	Allegro ♩ = 88; Allegretto vivace e sempre scherzando ♩. = 56; Adagio molto e mesto ♫ = 88, Molto cantabile ♪ = 88; Allegro ♩ = 126, Adagio ma non troppo ♪ = 69, Presto ♩ = 92
59/3	String Quartet in C major	Introduzione: Andante con moto ♩ = 69, Allegro vivace ♩ = 88; Andante con moto quasi Allegretto ♩. = 56; Menuetto grazioso ♩ = 116; Allegro molto o = 84
67	Symphony No. 5	Allegro con brio ♩ = 108; Andante con moto ♪ = 92; Allegro ♩. = 96; Allegro ♩ = 84, Presto o = 112
68	Symphony No. 6 (Pastoral)	Allegro ma non troppo ♩ = 66; Andante molto mosso ♩. = 50; Allegro ♩. = 108, a tempo Allegro ♩ = 132; Allegro ♩ = 80; Allegretto ♩. = 60
92	Symphony No. 7	Poco sostenuto ♩ = 69, Vivace ♩. = 104; Allegretto ♩ = 76; Presto ♩. = 132, Assai meno presto ♩. = 84; Allegro con brio ♩ = 72
95	String Quartet in F minor	Allegro con brio ♩ = 92; Allegretto ma non troppo ♩ = 66; Allegro assai vivace ma serioso ♩. = 69, Più allegro ♩. = 80; Larghetto espressivo ♪ = 56, Allegretto agitato ♩. = 92, Allegro o = 92
106	Piano Sonata ('Hammerklavier')	Allegro ♩ = 138; Scherzo ♩ = 80; Adagio sostenuto ♪ = 92; Largo ♫ = 76, Allegro risoluto ♩ = 144
125	Symphony No. 9 ('Choral')	Allegro ma non troppo un poco maestoso ♩ = 88; Molto vivace ♩. = 116, Presto o = 116; Adagio molto e cantabile ♩ = 60, Andante moderato ♩ = 63; Finale: Presto ♩. = 66, Allegro ma non troppo ♩ = 88, Allegro assai ♩ = 80, Allegro assai vivace. Alla Marcia ♩ = 84, Andante maestoso ♩ = 72, Adagio ma non troppo ma divoto ♩ = 60, Allegro energico e sempre ben marcato ♩. = 84, Allegro ma non tanto ♩ = 120, Prestissimo ♩ = 132, Maestoso ♩ = 60

What is more, there is the additional problem of tempo flexibility. Earlier in the period, steadiness of tempo was seen as an attribute. When the fifteen-year-old Mozart played a concert in Venice in 1771, he was praised for his attention to rhythm and metre. And the Viennese violinist Joseph Michael Böhm described the deaf Beethoven as following the bows of a string quartet so that 'he was able to judge the smallest fluctuations in tempo or rhythm and correct them immediately'. In a similar vein, Ferdinand Ries wrote that although Beethoven generally played his compositions impetuously, 'for the most part [he] stayed strictly in time, only infrequently pushing the tempo a little. Occasionally he would retard during a crescendo, which created a very beautiful and most remarkable effect'. Recent studies of Schubert's works, on the other hand, suggest that steadiness of tempo depended on genre. Most of the orchestral music, for example the 'Great C major' Symphony, apparently requires a steady beat, even from slow introductions to allegros. Yet this may not always be the case with his songs, where expression of the text is paramount; it has even been argued that Schubert's 'hairpin' signs, usually regarded as indications of dynamic, may reflect subtle tempo variations (this in spite of an eyewitness account that Schubert, in his songs, 'always kept the most strict and even time, except in the few places where he expressly indicated in writing a ritardando, morendo [or] accelerando'). In any event, excessive flexibility of tempo – apparently a characteristic fault of eighteenth-century singers, who were sometimes described as 'presumptuous' for thinking an orchestra should grind to a halt while he or she went off on an ornamental tangent – was considered bad taste, and tempo variations were almost always marked by composers, using terms such as *rallentando*, *stringendo*, *perdendosi*, *appassionato* and occasionally *espressivo* (which Beethoven, in the finale to his Violin Sonata Op. 96, follows with *a tempo*).

Discreet tempo rubato, on the other hand, was expected. Mozart described this in a letter of 1777 to his father: 'They all marvel that I always stay in strict time. They don't realize that tempo rubato in an adagio does not apply to the left hand'. This is not far from the description by Pier Francesco Tosi in 1723: 'when the Bass goes an exactly regular Pace, the other Part retards or anticipates in a singular manner, for the Sake of Expression, but after That returns to its exactness, to be guided by the Bass'. Ultimately, it is necessary to create a persuasive beat, although this often requires a paradoxical mixture of precision and flexibility that avoids both mechanical regularity and caprice.

The third of Rousseau's factors for determining tempo, character, is not only the most important but also the most difficult to pin down. At the time the *Dictionnaire* was published, character was related to 'characteristic': that is, it concerned movements deriving from well-established types, such as minuets, marches, or gavottes. Today such 'types' are often described as 'topics' (see Chapter 1 'Historical Background', pp. 13–14). By the 1780s, however, unity of expression (and hence 'type') had given way to a kaleidoscopic array of contrasting gestures, often within a single phrase; and these gestures so transcend their models in complexity that their original 'meanings' had to all intents and purposes been shunted aside in favour of more complex and individuated interaction. What, then, is the 'character' of a work? For Schumann, Mozart's Symphony in G minor K. 550 represented 'Grecian lightness and grace'; for some mid-twentieth-century conductors, however, it seems to have been a ponderous dirge. Choice of tempo is therefore crucial in expressing character, which is only partly 'in' the work – mostly it is 'in' the performer.

Among the eighteenth- and early nineteenth-century sources that eloquently draw together notions of tempo and character, Heinrich Christoph Koch's *Musikalisches Lexikon* of 1802 is of special importance. Some of his comments are as follows:

> Largo, actually signifies broad or expanded; this term indicates the most familiar slow tempo, which accommodates itself only to those sentiments which should be expressed with solemn slowness. With respect to performance, the comments given in the article 'Adagio' must be observed even more carefully in the Largo...
>
> Adagio, moderately slowly...calls for a particularly finely-drawn performance, partly because the slow tempo emphasizes every turn which does not correspond to the ruling sentiment, and partly because the music will become boring and unpleasant if the tempo is not maintained with sufficient momentum...
>
> Andante, moving, walking. This term indicates a pace midway between fast and slow. When this term is not used for characteristic pieces, such as processions, marches, etc., then it applies to pieces in which the sentiments of calmness, quiet and contentment are embodied. Here the notes should neither drag nor blend into each other much as in the Adagio, nor be as accentuated and separated as in the Allegro...
>
> Allegro, quick...moderately quick tempo... The performance of an allegro calls for a firm tone quality, a simple and clear delivery, the notes themselves in this tempo being connected only when expressly indicated or when a prominent cantabile section appears; otherwise, the notes are generally separated rather decisively...
>
> Presto, rapid, quick...the quickest category of tempo... In purely instrumental music the presto calls for a fleeting and light, yet straightforward delivery; in opera, on the other hand, where this tempo is used for sentiments of the greatest intensity, more vigour must be expressed in the sharper accentuation of the tones, and the clarity of the performance must not thereby suffer.

The best and most straightforward explanation of tempo markings is probably Leopold Mozart's. Unlike all other early theorists, he lists only the most basic tempos; everything else must be understood as indicating character. It is therefore implicit in Leopold's formulation, and presumably in Wolfgang's practice as well as the practice of his contemporaries, that the performer has considerable leeway in choosing tempos that are both technically feasible and characteristic. A convenient starting point, mentioned by both Leopold Mozart and Türk, is to base tempos in the first instance on the shortest note-values or on a particularly important passage. Effective performance and character are key elements – Mozart is alleged to have said about the overture to *Le nozze di Figaro* (The Marriage of Figaro): 'where fire is lacking...speed cannot add anything'.

Articulation and phrasing

Articulation encompasses several aspects of performance, including the degree of separation between notes and the degree of emphasis they are given. It is notated by slurs, dots and strokes, rests and even the rhythmic values assigned to the notes themselves. Eighteenth-century treatises give full coverage of the subject, and understandably so: articulation lies at the heart of performance in this repertoire.

Most eighteenth-century sources agree that in the absence of a specific staccato or slur sign, notes are slightly separated from each other and played somewhat shorter than notated. This rule is prescribed by C. P. E. Bach, Quantz and Leopold Mozart. But there is little agreement on the amount by which notes should be 'underplayed'; C. P. E. Bach advocates reducing notes to half their value or less, while Türk gives a variety of options:

Unless otherwise marked, then, separation is the norm, at least until about 1800. Legato, on the other hand, is less common, and needed to be indicated in the score. Sometimes the word itself is written; usually, however, it is marked by slurs binding together two, three, four or more notes. It is unusual, though not unheard of, for slurs to cross bar-lines. In this regard, care has to be exercised when playing from modern editions, many of which preserve nineteenth-century ways of thinking about staccato, separation and legato; frequently they lengthen slurs where the original sources have unequivocally short slurs:

Ex. 2.1. D. G. Türk, *Clavierschule* (1789): options for shortening written crotchets.

If separation is the norm, and legato (almost) always specifically marked, then what is to be made of staccato dots and strokes, which by this way of thinking seem unnecessary and superfluous? The simple answer is that a staccato is not a staccato after all but something else. Indeed, it is likely that Mozart never wrote a staccato dot in his life except in one specific situation: dots under slurs, usually in string or wind parts but sometimes in piano music as well, indicating *portato* (literally 'dragged'), a special kind of articulation in which successive notes are taken in one bow (or the keyboard equivalent of a bow stroke), but with a slight separation between

Ex. 2.2. W. A. Mozart, Trio in E major for piano, violin and cello K. 542, 1788: second movement, Andante grazioso, piano RH, bb. 1–8. Articulation from the nineteenth-century Breitkopf & Härtel edition shown above the stave, and articulation from the autograph score shown below the stave.

them (see Chapter 4 'Strings', p. 58). Instead, as a careful study of his autographs and performing copies shows, Mozart always wrote strokes. (This simple fact was not recognized even as late as the 1950s and 60s, and is frequently not reflected in editions even today.)

The staccato dot, as distinguished from the contemporaneous stroke or later marcato wedge, originated as a nineteenth-century typographical convention: forced to choose signs representing the increasingly detailed articulations marked by composers in their works, publishers opted for fixed meanings that have now become standard. Beethoven was aware of this burgeoning convention, although evidence of his own usage of dots and strokes is contradictory: there are instances where they seem to be identical, but others where a distinction is apparently intended – in a late letter to the violinist Holz he wrote, 'Where a dot occurs above a note no stroke should replace it, and vice-versa'. For Mozart and Haydn, however, there was no difference, just as there was no difference for the majority of contemporaneous theorists (Türk, in 1789, noted that some writers saw dots and strokes as separate signs, without necessarily sanctioning that view).

No doubt one reason for this is that the stroke was not fixed in its meaning. It could indicate not only accent and separation but also phrase endings or a countermanding of normal expectations. This is rare in Mozart, but sometimes found in Haydn: for example in the finale of the Sonata Hob. XVI/49, where strokes shift the emphasis to the downbeats (Ex. 2.3). In Mozart (see Ex. 2.4), strokes are found over the four-note

Ex. 2.3. J. Haydn, Sonata in E flat major Hob. XVI/49, 1789–90: third movement, Tempo di Minuet, bb. 1–2.

Ex. 2.4. Different uses of the stroke from W. A. Mozart (a) Symphony No. 41 K. 551, 1788: fourth movement, Molto allegro, violin I, bb. 9–12;

semibreve motto in the finale of the 'Jupiter' Symphony, indicating emphasis (a); in numerous passages where repeated notes in an otherwise legato passage, usually conjunct in motion, need clear separation and articulation (b); and in combination with slurs to set off the final elements of repeated arpeggiation or other sequential figures (c).

(b) String Quartet in C major K. 465, 1785: fourth movement, Allegro molto, violin I, bb. 55–7;
(c) String Quartet in B flat major K. 458, 1784: first movement, Allegro vivace assai, violin I, b. 1.

Strokes also function as a sign to vary textures between the hands in piano music (as in Ex. 2.5); and occasionally they are mated with other markings to form a composite sign (see 'Dynamics' below). In cases such as these, it is clear that the strokes do not stand alone, but function in tandem with other signs to shape a figure and to emphasize its beginning, middle or end.

As a general rule, the first note of a slur is taken more strongly than the notes that follow. This is in keeping with eighteenth-century notions of

phrasing and 'good' notes, that is, certain downbeats: in a four-bar phrase, for example, the downbeats of the first and third bars are 'good' and require a stronger accent, while the downbeats of the second and fourth bars are less emphasized. Whole phrases, and indeed successions of phrases, should also be thought of as having 'good' bars, as Türk pointed out, so that, in effect, some notes, and some bars, are 'better' than others:

Ex. 2.5. J. Haydn, Sonata in A major Hob. XVI/30, 1774–6: first movement, Allegro, bb. 174–183.

> Every note that begins a period must have a still stronger accent than that of the *usual* good note. To be sure, such notes that begin a section should be accented more or less according to the extent of the section to follow; that is, after a perfect cadence, the beginning note must be more strongly marked than after a half-cadence or after a simple pause.

The succession of 'good' and 'better' notes and bars, together with other aspects of articulation and dynamics, gives shape to a movement, resulting in a hierarchy of gestures that in the hands of Haydn, Mozart, Beethoven or Schubert reflects the larger architecture of their works. But it would be incorrect to assume that the composer's overall conception necessarily demands uniformity of articulation, either among parts in ensemble or orchestral music, or between parallel passages in all kinds of works. Mozart, in both his scores and performing parts, rarely writes articulation for the horns, for example, even when they double, or nearly double, the oboes. And most modern editions of the String Quartet K. 421 standardize the articulation of bar 3 (and the parallel passage) of the Andante to eliminate apparent discrepancies between the first and second violin parts, even though Mozart's autograph (Ex. 2.6), and the first edition prepared

Ex. 2.6. W. A. Mozart, String Quartet in D minor K. 421, 1783, autograph score: second movement, Andante, bb. 1–8.

Ex. 2.7. Beethoven,
Sonata in E flat major
Op. 81a, 1809–10:
first movement,
Adagio – Allegro
(a) bb. 46–7;
(b) bb. 138–9.

under his supervision, are absolutely consistent in their differing articulations. Beethoven provides similar, thought-provoking examples, such as the first movement of the Piano Sonata Op. 81a (Ex. 2.7), where the slurring of bars 46–7 in the exposition (a) is 'reversed' at bars 138–9 in the recapitulation (b).

These general observations notwithstanding, there is a difference between music of the earlier and later parts of the Classical period. Carl Czerny, in the autobiographical sketch that he wrote in 1842, refers to fundamental changes in the style of piano playing between Mozart's time and his own: like Beethoven, who described Mozart's pianism as 'choppy', he drew a distinction between the earlier, more detached style and the more legato style then current. In part, this difference resulted from the increased importance of broad, sweeping melodies in music at the turn of the century. And it was a natural result of changes to the playing techniques and construction of different instruments: in string playing, for example, the fundamental stroke of the pre-Tourte, or eighteenth-century, bow was non-legato. But this does not mean that Mozart or Haydn played in a manner inappropriate to the music at hand: after all, Mozart repeatedly stressed the desirability of a cantabile, 'singing' quality in instrumental performance, as well as 'naturalness'. On the contrary, it is chiefly a matter of interaction between style and technique: the greater melodic continuity of nineteenth-century music, together with changes in the construction of musical instruments, gave rise to, and facilitated, long lines; for Mozart and Haydn, however, singing melodies are played off against busy motivic and rhythmic gestures that, taken together, constitute the fabric of a work. An important marker of these differences is a greater or lesser degree of detached articulation.

Rhythmic alteration

The performance of dotted rhythms may have involved some shortening of the shorter note-values, as was common in the Baroque. This is especially the case for 'overture' passages in archaic style, whether in solo music or in orchestral passages such as the introductions to Haydn's Symphony No. 104 and Mozart's 'Linz' Symphony K. 425. In fact, the two authentic sources for the 'Linz' give the rhythm of the opening differently: one, a copy made in Salzburg in 1784, has ♪ 𝄾 ♪ throughout the bar, while the other, which dates from Vienna in 1786, has ♪ 𝄾 ♪ . Similarly, it is unclear whether dotted rhythms performed simultaneously with triplets should be 'assimilated', adjusted to fit the triplets, or over-dotted to emphasize the difference between the two parts – a particularly vexed question in the performance of Schubert. However, two-against-three rhythms,

unusual in the Baroque period, were more common in the Classical: Türk
described them as 'a beauty to which one has to grow accustomed'.

Dynamics

Although during this period notated dynamics ranged from *pianissimo* to
fortissimo, *forte* and *piano* were by far the most frequently used – indeed,
sometimes they were the only dynamics. But they do not necessarily
represent a continuation of the Baroque tradition of so-called terraced
dynamics. On the contrary, while specific signs often represent sudden
dynamic change, they just as frequently represent dynamic contour.

Some cases are unambiguously clear. In Haydn's Piano Sonata Hob.
XVI/36 (Ex. 2.8), for instance, there can be no question about the sudden

Ex. 2.8. J. Haydn,
Sonata in C sharp
minor Hob. XVI/36,
?c.1770–75: first
movement,
Moderato, bb. 1–7.

decrease in dynamics at bar 2: the unison opening gives way to a single
note, the phrase is entirely different in character from the opening, and the
continuation shows that the *g♯'* is not merely part of a filler (which could
imply a gradual decrease in dynamics) but the beginning of a new motif,
thereby demanding an articulative, dynamic change. But how are the
dynamics in bars 3 and 4 of Mozart's B minor Adagio K. 540 (Ex. 2.9) to be
interpreted? As a sudden dynamic shift in mid-phrase, or as a gradual
decrescendo?

Ex. 2.9.
W. A. Mozart, Adagio
in B minor K. 540,
1788: bb. 1–5.

Particular attention must be paid to the symbol *fp*, which has a variety of meanings. About mid-century this sign was often combined with a stroke (see 'Articulation and phrasing' above) and a specific beaming, ♪ ♫ ♫ , not to signify any particular dynamic level, but to represent an *fp* accent. Later it was often used in the modern sense familiar from Beethoven's sonatas. But there is one remarkable case, from Mozart's Trio K. 498, for piano, clarinet and viola, that shows just how difficult the sign is to interpret. There are two authentic sources for the opening of this work: Mozart's autograph score, and the incipit (quotation of the opening bars) in the thematic catalogue of his works that he began in February 1784. The opening paragraph of the first movement is an antecedent–consequent (or question-and-answer) phrase arranged in four two-bar sub-phrases (see Ex. 2.10 which reproduces only the first two). The unison opening bars in this movement are taken by the piano and viola, while the harmonized 'response' belongs to the keyboard alone. In his autograph, Mozart writes *fp* on the first downbeat. In his thematic catalogue, however, the *forte* stands alone, and the *piano* does not occur until the end of the second bar. This is not merely a minor difference in dynamic placement; on the contrary, the two sources represent differing accounts of the work's opening, one in which the strong downbeat is immediately countermanded by the *piano* continuation of the triadic figure, and another in which the opening gesture sweeps its way through the first bar and a half. In short, Mozart seems to provide two different *performances* – or is it three: could the notation also represent a diminuendo? After all, the two notations mean essentially the same thing: begin loudly and finish softly. The only real difference is that one formulation gives the information all at once, while the other roughly indicates dynamic end-points. (It is a good idea, by the way, to check original sources if at all possible. Modern editions frequently conflate as *fp* forte and *piano* signs that occur in quick succession – sometimes at the distance of no more than a crotchet or quaver – when in fact they are intended to be separate. In doing so, they not only prescribe a specific style of performance but also rob performers of valuable information and, what's worse, the right to decide for themselves.)

Ex. 2.10.
W. A. Mozart, Trio in E flat major for piano, clarinet and viola K. 498, 1786: first movement, Andante, bb. 1–4.

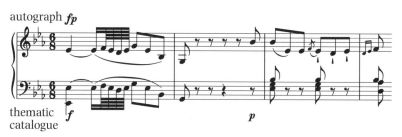

The frequency of notated – as opposed to performed – dynamics in eighteenth-century music depends in large part on both the genre and the type of source. The autographs of Mozart's piano sonatas, for example, are relatively free of dynamic signs; the first editions produced under his direction, however, are generously notated (no doubt the difference arises from the intended broad public dissemination of the prints, as opposed to the more private nature of the composer's score). The piano concertos are even more sparingly notated – but in this instance there are few early authorized editions, and so Mozart's dynamic intentions remain largely unknown. It can be assumed, however, that in performance Mozart used the full range of available dynamic gestures and nuances, even if they are not marked in his scores (or in modern editions). Indeed, this is generally true of most genres of the 1780s and 90s, including all sorts of vocal, orchestral and ensemble music. It was not until the nineteenth century that composers included abundant dynamic marks in their scores.

Beyond indicating accent or relative levels of loud and soft, dynamics also serve to articulate the musical drama of a movement or piece. Sometimes the effect is localized, and refers to a single phrase or paragraph of a work: the opening of Mozart's String Quartet in G major K. 387, with its successions of *forte* and *piano*, is only one example (Ex. 2.11). Do not be misled, however, by analogies between musical dynamics and stress in language. It seems quaint to us now, but an article in *The Musical Times* in 1927 took Mozart to task for his 'unnatural' dynamics in this passage, arguing:

> try to recite the first couplet of Goldsmith's 'Deserted Village' thus (shouting the words printed in capitals and whispering the words printed small): NEAR YONDER COPSE WHERE once the garden smiled, AND STILL WHERE MANY A garden flower grows wild.

But what is more profitable? To criticize composers for not writing as if music were a poem, or to ask what *musical* reasons they might have had for notating their works as they did? This example repays close scrutiny in any case: it is clearly built on rapid changes of dynamics that at the same time require careful nuancing. Note, for example, the succession of *piano* signs in bars 4 and 7 without an intervening *forte*.

Ex. 2.11.
W. A. Mozart, String Quartet in G major K. 387, 1782: first movement, Allegro vivace assai, bb. 1–10.

In other instances the importance of dynamics extends across a broader time span: the first movement of Beethoven's 'Eroica' Symphony, for example, includes a single *ppp* – the first in any of his symphonies – in the violins at bar 394. No doubt this was to ensure the audibility of the famous horn dissonance; but beyond that it says something about the shape of the movement as a whole. Dynamics therefore function as an integral part of long-range musical construction. Performers should not only take this into account when planning their interpretations but also, at the level of the phrase or paragraph, gratefully accept the frequent absence of detailed dynamics, which brings with it the responsibility to shape a dramatic and personalized interpretation.

Ornamentation

Ornamentation is also a large and difficult topic: exactly when and how to ornament a passage is by no means always clear. There are some unequivocal instances where ornamentation is expected, including repeated sections and da capo reprises; composer's manuscripts, or other good sources including first and early authorized editions, often provide just this kind of information. When Mozart published his piano sonatas during the 1780s he frequently added ornamentation which is otherwise lacking in

Ex. 2.12.
W. A. Mozart, Sonata in F major K. 332, 1781–3: second movement, Adagio, bb. 21–6.

his autographs: one example is a passage in the slow movement of K. 332 (Ex. 2.12). (Most good modern editions of the sonatas also include Mozart's ornamentation.)

Yet this particular constellation of sources, texts and documentary evidence is peculiar to the solo piano music. The situation is different, for example, with the concertos, where Mozart's notation is skeletal at best: because he had no expectation that they would be printed and disseminated, he apparently did not feel compelled to write out ornamentation that he improvised in performance. Nevertheless, it is clear that he did improvise and ornament in many passages that, seen only on the page, look bare. In a letter to his father on 9 June 1784, he wrote that his sister Nannerl was 'quite right in saying that there is something missing in the solo passage in C in the Andante of the Concerto in D [K. 451]. I will supply the deficiency as soon as possible'. Ex. 2.13 gives the passage as it appears in Mozart's autograph and the elaboration that he later sent to his sister. Examples also survive from Mozart's hand showing ornamentation for vocal music: see Ex. 6.8 in Chapter 6 'Singing', p. 85.

Ex. 2.13.
W. A. Mozart, Piano Concerto in D major K. 451, 1784: second movement, Andante, bb. 56–63.

Ornamentation was generally practised, as in these examples, by solo performers; but it was perhaps expected also in some ensemble works, such as Mozart's Quartet for oboe and strings K. 370 with its concertante wind part. It was normally frowned upon in orchestral music – though the very fact that contemporary writers made a point of condemning the practice shows that it was quite common. In fact, there are instances where ornamentation by orchestral players might be welcome, for example in passages in Mozart's piano concertos where a single wind player engages in playful dialogue with the soloist.

There are no standard rules for realizing and performing Classical ornamentation, since, among other things, the period encompasses a transition from the symbolic notation of the late Baroque to the fully written-out ornamentation of the Romantic period. Nor was the realization of specific melodic ornaments, as opposed to improvised ornamentation, standardized. The trill, for example, could be long or short, begin on the upper note (the usual practice) or on the main note (depending on the approach to the trill and whether the main note is dissonant or consonant), or have additional ornamental turns at the beginning or end. (Leopold Mozart describes four kinds of trills appropriate to various tempos and characters: slow, medium, fast and accelerating.) Similarly, dissonant appoggiaturas – usually played on the beat – could also be long or short; in general the value of the appoggiatura is subtracted from the main note. A particularly problematic case, however, is the prosodic appoggiatura: one view is that any line ending on a repeated note and followed by a rest or punctuation mark (a so-called 'feminine' ending) must be articulated by an appoggiatura of some kind; another view is that contemporary writings, including works by Salieri, Telemann, Marpurg, Mancini and Gluck, legitimize note repetition as well. (For a discussion of the appoggiatura in vocal music, see Chapter 6 'Singing', pp. 81–3.) The following example shows ways of realizing some standard ornaments, but these should be considered examples only.

Ex. 2.14. Suggested realization of ornaments, based on D. G. Türk, *Clavierschule* (1789/1802). Notice that the small notes do not always add up to the correct number of beats as in modern notation.

Long appoggiaturas

Short appoggiaturas

contrariwise, here long

Largo

Trills without Nachschlag (conclusion)

written

Allegro assai **Alla breve** **Andante**

performed

Trills with Nachschlag

written

performed
mostly *also*

Pralltriller

written

performed

Mordents

Acciaccaturas

Battement

Turns

Other types of ornament are not usually thought of as such, but were considered so by the eighteenth century: these include vibrato and the *messa di voce* or swell (see also Chapter 4 'Strings', pp. 52–3 and 59–60, and Chapter 5 'Wind Instruments', pp. 70–71). For all their ubiquitousness now, both were relatively infrequent during the eighteenth century and used only in suitable places, usually long held notes. Leopold Mozart wrote disparagingly of violinists who 'tremble consistently on each note as if they had the palsy', and in a letter to his son on 28 May 1778 he described the oboist Carlo Besozzi as having a '*messa di voce* that was too frequent for my taste and has the same melancholy effect on me as the tones of the [glass] harmonica, for it produces almost the same kind of sound'. For Wolfgang Mozart, these effects were appropriate only when they were 'natural'. He wrote to his father on 12 June 1778:

> Meissner [a Salzburg singer]...has the bad habit of making his voice tremble at times, turning a note that should be sustained into distinct crotchets, or even quavers – and this I never could endure in him. Really, it is a detestable habit and one that is quite contrary to nature. The human voice trembles naturally – but in its own way – and only to such a degree that the effect is beautiful. Such is the nature of the voice; and people imitate it not only on wind instruments, but on stringed instruments too and even on the keyboard. But the moment the proper limit is overstepped, it is no longer beautiful – because it is contrary to nature.

Piano pedalling must count as an ornament too, although pedal markings are rarely found during this period. In all of Haydn's piano music the only authentic pedal indication is found in the first movement of the Sonata Hob. XVI/50; the evidence of contemporary pianos, as well as local performance practices, suggests that this refers to the damper pedal, rather than the *una corda*. Mozart's works lack pedal indications altogether, although his piano did include levers for sustaining either half of the keyboard; one passage that seems unequivocally to require pedal is found at the end of the second movement of the Sonata in D major K. 311:

Ex. 2.15.
W. A. Mozart, Sonata in D major K. 311, 1777: second movement, Andante con espressione, bb. 83–90.

Similarly, slurred Alberti bass passages were probably meant to be performed with the bottom note sustained throughout; this is the so-called finger pedal (see again Ex. 2.15). For Beethoven, pedal indications are more numerous, beginning with the Sonata Op. 26, where he writes *senza sordino* and *con sordino* (dampers off, dampers on); from the 'Waldstein' onwards he uses the standard 'Ped.' symbol (Ex. 2.16). (For more on piano pedalling, see Chapter 3 'Keyboard'.)

Ex. 2.16. Beethoven, 'Waldstein' Sonata Op. 53, 1803–4, autograph score: third movement, Allegretto moderato, bb. 251–8. Beethoven indicates the lifting of the pedal by O.

Fermatas, lead-ins and cadenzas

In general, a fermata (⌒) is an invitation to ornament, briefly or at length depending on the musical context and the whim of the performer (although good taste normally militates against excessively long fermatas). Numerous examples can be found in the finales of Mozart's piano concertos; in the first movements, of course, the potent 6-4 chord at the end demands a cadenza – several of which survive for the Viennese concertos (these are good models for improvising cadenzas in those cases where none is extant). More problematic are cases where a real or implied fermata must be accommodated to the musical drama. In Mozart's Quintet K. 452 for piano and wind an improvised lead-in at the end of the exposition, returning to the opening of the work, seems feasible at the first blush. But the effect, in this particular instance, would be to diminish the drama of the development, which begins with the same motif but a 3rd lower. A nearly identical dramatic construct occurs in the first movement of the 'Hoffmeister' String Quartet K. 499, which, given that it is an ensemble work, is unlikely to have included ornamentation of this kind. Accordingly, the introduction of lead-ins and other types of ornamentation, while clearly desirable in some circumstances, should by no means be an automatic response to a fermata.

Putting it all together

There comes a moment in every good story when the threads of the narrative are drawn together, when the twists and turns of the plot are finally resolved. Yet that hardly seems possible in this instance. Ornamentation, it seems, is often called for but sometimes an unnecessary intrusion; strokes may indicate accent, separation or phrasing; dynamics are signs of large-scale structure as well as volume; tempos are sometimes variable, sometimes not; and local practices in Vienna, Paris, Berlin and London may or may not apply across the broad spectrum of late eighteenth- and early nineteenth-century musical culture. What is more, it is rarely, if ever, the case that different aspects of notation and interpretation function independently of each other.

One final consideration has what is arguably the most profound effect on a performance: that is, our view of a composer's personality. Haydn, as we all know, was a purveyor of surprise and wit, Schubert a gentle, lyrical soul, Beethoven a titanic struggler against life, and Mozart a divinely inspired genius, a paragon of symmetry, balance and grace. But what if we see these composers differently? What if we see them as more than one-dimensional? In that case, notation takes on an entirely different aspect – and it invariably leads to an all-embracing view of the various elements of notation and performance. By way of example, let us take a close look at a passage (Ex. 2.17) from the Mozart C minor Fantasia K. 475, composed in Vienna in 1785 to accompany the C minor Piano Sonata K. 457.

In the B flat Andantino section, at bars 86, 87, 94, 95 and 114, both the autograph and first edition (published under Mozart's supervision) give the held inner voice f' (or f) as a minim (see also the F, G and A in bars 118, 120 and 122 – part of a rising sequence based on the same figure). All modern editions, however, give the reading of the inner voice as either a crotchet tied to a quaver or a dotted crotchet, followed by a quaver rest. Why is this?

Ex. 2.17.
W. A. Mozart,
Fantasia in C minor
K. 475, 1785
(a) autograph score,
bb. 86–124;
(b) first edition
(1785), bb. 86–124;
(c) modern edition,
bb. 86–7, 94–5, 114
and 118–22.

(a)

The simple answer seems to be that in the absence of Mozart's auto-graph, which was for many years lost, editors believed that the duration of the inner voice had to correspond to the two outer voices; this was Mozart's 'style', his personality – the held-on minim would be untidy, unruly, un-Mozartian. Accordingly, the reading in these bars, even though it is consist-ently a minim in the edition authorized by the composer himself, was changed. The rediscovery in 1989 of Mozart's autograph, which is ident-ical to the first edition, did little to improve matters: new editions continue to appear with the 'traditional', rather than the autograph, version. Apparently our image of Mozart has not changed much since the nine-teenth century: he is still a paragon of balance and grace.

Nevertheless, although it is clear that Mozart wrote a minim, it hardly suffices to note that his score and the first edition agree. The passage is problematic at best, a moment of possibly unresolved instability of both notation and performance: the autograph shows that the original notation of the second and third beats in the upper voice of bar 86 was a crotchet followed by a quaver rest and a dotted semiquaver rest, with both upper voices sounding in tandem to the end of the second crotchet of the bar. The lower line, too, was originally conceived to last two crotchets: when he changed the right hand, Mozart added flags to the c' and $e\flat'$ of the left hand, making quavers out of what originally had been crotchets, and interpolating a quaver rest before the crotchet rest at the end of the bar. At the same time, however, Mozart did not make one other apparently neces-sary, and typical, change: where he writes polyphonically, each voice has its own rests. Here, however, the rests are construed as if each had repre-sented only one voice, lasting a crotchet and a half; by rights, the minim should be followed by a crotchet rest alone, not the quaver and crotchet rests demanded by the outer voices.

It seems unlikely, but, given these inconsistencies and apparently partial changes, could Mozart have intended, yet failed, to correct the inner-voice f' as well as the rests? Or does the fact that the reading appears in two authentic sources mean that it is 'correct'? Furthermore, what is to be made of bars 90 and 106, where the inner voice is not held? In fact, the contexts are not identical: in bars 86–7 and 94–5, where the theme is given a relatively stable bar-and-a-half statement in two complementary parts (or at the rising sequence at the end of the section, which still retains the complementarity), the minim appears; but in other passages, with their rhythmic diminutions, harmonic instability and forward thrust, Mozart writes a crotchet tied to a quaver. It is a distinction that is consistently applied throughout the Andantino. The problem, then, is not merely editor-ial but one of meaning and performance. And choosing a 'solution' to what at first glance seems to be merely a notational irregularity depends in no small part on perceptions of Mozart's style in general, and the role of this particular passage within the Fantasia as a whole.

At times – good examples include the slow movements of the G minor and D minor string quintets or the slow introduction to the 'Prague' Symphony – Mozart's manipulation of texture and textural contrast threatens to overwhelm other aspects of a piece, including both harmony and melody. The rhythmically extended f' in the Andantino of the C minor

Fantasia may be just such an example: the inner-voice pedal sounds through the notated silence of the other parts, penetrating the spare textures, drawing the ear to the literal 'heart' of the passage. And not only does it demand a performance decision with respect to voicing, emphasis and length; it forces on the performer two additional decisions. One of them concerns tempo: for the f' to sound after the other voices, the Andantino must be taken fairly quickly, otherwise the note will already have expired.

The other decision is rhythmic, concerning the re-entry of the upper-most voice with an upbeat demisemiquaver: does it follow in strict tempo, or is some period of silence or hesitation necessary after the fading of the inner voice? If the latter, then the beginning of the bar must be taken quickly but the ending distended, threatening the metrical stability of the passage. Seen in this way, the Andantino suddenly takes on an ambiguous function within the context of the Fantasia as a whole: for all its tonal solidity – surely one of its most important attributes – it nevertheless may be essentially unstable. Accordingly, it too becomes fantasy-like, vaguely reminiscent of the irregularities that characterize the unstable opening of the work.

Incidentally, it needs to be added that choice of instrument, eighteenth-century or modern, is also a crucial performance decision: the interpretation of notation, and its realization in performance, depends to a great extent on the characteristics of any particular instrument. In the Mozart Andantino, the f' is especially likely to expire quickly when played on a piano of the time, unless the tempo is kept moving. On the modern grand piano, the tempo has to be slower to bring out the prolonged f', since the sound of the outer voices lasts much longer.

All told, then, even a single moment of notation – a minim f' or a crotchet tied to a quaver – can raise questions about the work as a whole, forcing the performer to think about choice of instrument, rhythm, accent, articulation, tempo, tempo variation and, ultimately, expression (*Affekt*). And as is clear, no single one of these elements functions in isolation from the others. What is more, performance decisions will ultimately be based, at least in part, on a perception of the author's compositional persona. Is Mozart a paragon of symmetry, balance and regularity? Or is he self-consciously aware, disruptively exploiting to every advantage what is the essence of the 'Classical style', the notion of contrast?

This decision, which only the performer can make, bears on the interpretation in performance of virtually every notational detail of a piece. And it is a difficult choice, ultimately raising more questions than it answers. (What could be more confusing than to realize that sometimes notation means what it says, but sometimes it does not?) One thing, however, is certain: all notation means something. It is a call to interpretative action, an invitation to exercise critical judgement, to think – and finally to *perform*.

David Ward

Keyboard

The piano and its music

The Classical period saw enormous changes in the style and content of music, and this is particularly evident in the field of keyboard music. The most obvious change occurred in the instruments themselves. At the beginning of the period the piano, although at least sixty years old, was only just beginning to be accepted as a viable alternative to the harpsichord and the clavichord; but by 1830 it was the only stringed keyboard instrument still in use. In these seventy years the piano itself underwent enormous changes, from something that sounded not very different from a harpsichord to an instrument of power and range, capable of coping with the demands of the late sonatas by Beethoven and Schubert – but still a very different instrument from the one we know today.

There were also many changes in the music written for keyboard. This period saw the rise of the sonata and 'sonata form'. In the first half of the eighteenth century J. S. Bach wrote suites, partitas, toccatas, variations, and preludes and fugues. His second son, Carl Philipp Emanuel, wrote sonatas and many shorter pieces, especially rondos and fantasies; his youngest son, Johann Christian, also wrote sonatas, which we know he played in London on a 'square' piano (more on this later). Haydn, who was an admirer of C. P. E. Bach and greatly influenced by him, wrote a wonderful series of sixty keyboard sonatas, the latest of which were certainly conceived for the 'pianoforte'. Mozart, also an admirer of C. P. E. but closer to and more influenced by J. C., was a unique performer on the piano and left a remarkable addition to the repertoire: first and foremost his twenty-seven piano concertos, but also eighteen sonatas, fifteen sets of variations and many shorter pieces.

A significant development was the inclusion of the new instrument in chamber music. The harpsichord had been used as an indispensable accompaniment for centuries, but this was mostly in the form of the basso continuo, in which the performer had to 'realize' the keyboard part from a figured bass. With the rise of the more expressive piano, the keyboard became an equal partner in sonatas, trios and so on. The early 'fortepianos' (as pianos of the period are usually called) were admirably suited to ensemble playing, allowing a much better balance of textures with the strings or wind of the time than can be achieved on modern instruments.

The end of the eighteenth century and the beginning of the nineteenth saw the rise of the virtuoso composer-pianist, which not only meant an increase in technical brilliance but also had a considerable effect on the size and construction of the instruments. An example of this is Muzio

Clementi, who was a maker of pianos as well as a fine pianist and an important composer.

Beethoven was renowned for the brilliance and expressiveness of his playing in his early years, before deafness prevented him from performing in public. Throughout his composing career he made full use of the instrument in concertos, chamber music and solo works, always pushing it to its limits. To play his *Sonate pathétique* Op. 13 (1797–8) on an instrument of the time is to become aware of how the piano *had* to grow in order to accommodate the new music. Beethoven's thirty-two sonatas cover an extraordinary range of emotion and spirituality, and they are endlessly inventive in their musical language and technical demands. He also wrote many sets of variations and shorter pieces.

As an antidote to the large and often weighty sonata, many composers began to write shorter pieces, often bearing fanciful or romantic titles such as Impromptu, Moment Musical or Nocturne. The Irish composer and pianist John Field was the originator of the nocturne, and Schubert wrote

two sets of impromptus and one set of *Moments musicaux*. Schubert left a wonderful legacy of piano music, not only in his shorter pieces and his longer (some very long) sonatas but also in the accompaniments to his songs. The art of piano accompaniment could almost be said to begin with these beautiful and imaginative piano parts, which are still a challenge for the finest pianists.

Mozart was the first great composer to write a substantial number of sonatas for piano duet (four hands at one keyboard); later Schubert composed some magnificent four-hand music. Duet playing became increasingly popular among amateur pianists, creating a market not only for original duets but also for arrangements of chamber and orchestral works, which allowed a larger audience to experience this music at first hand.

So it is clear that these seventy years saw the rise of the piano to the dominant position which it still holds today. As the instrument grew in popularity and became more readily available in many shapes and sizes, so more and more people began to play it, and the early nineteenth century saw an enormous increase in instruction books and collections of music attractive to the amateur pianist. The music industry was in full swing!

The instruments

Before looking more closely at the piano itself, let us consider briefly the two main keyboard instruments which preceded it, and with which it coexisted for about a hundred years. The harpsichord is an instrument on which the

strings vibrate by being plucked; it has a clear and bright sound with a very clean and open texture. It was used extensively for about 300 years as a solo instrument or as accompaniment, providing a marvellous foil in particular to the more expressive voice and violin. Its great limitation, however, is that its mechanism allows the strings to be displaced by a uniform amount only, and therefore it is not possible to vary the tone or the intensity of the sound with the fingers.

By contrast, the smaller clavichord is a highly sensitive instrument, with a very simple action. A small metal rod or 'tangent' is pressed against the

Fig. 3.1. Double-manual harpsichord by Jacob and Abraham Kirkman, London, 1776.

strings, acting both as an activator and as a stop. The point where the tangent touches the string is one end of the vibrating length of the string. As the tangent remains in touch with the string until the key is released, it is possible to effect a vibrato, or *Bebung*, by gently moving the key up and down to vary the pitch of the note. Because the tangent strikes the string, the speed of impact can be varied and consequently the volume. The clavichord is thus more closely related to the piano than the harpsichord. Its limitation is that it produces a very small sound.

Fig. 3.2. Clavichord by Christian Gotthelf Hoffmann, Ronneburg, Saxony, 1784.

So on the one hand there was the powerful and brilliant harpsichord, and on the other the gentle and expressive clavichord; and it could be said that the piano arose to combine the qualities of these two instruments. It is generally accepted that the piano was invented in Italy by Bartolomeo Cristofori (1655–1732) in about 1700, but in fact many experiments with a striking action had taken place prior to this. However, Cristofori's instruments were the first to attract any serious attention. He developed an elaborate 'escapement action' (Fig. 3.3) which, when the key (C) was depressed, caused a small hammer (O) to be thrown at the strings (A) and to rebound immediately, leaving the strings free to vibrate. When the key was released a damper (R) came into contact with the strings, thereby stopping the vibration. This is the basis of modern piano action, although the piano was

Fig. 3.3. S. Maffei, diagram of Cristofori's piano action from *Giornale de' letterati d'Italia*, Vol. v (1711).

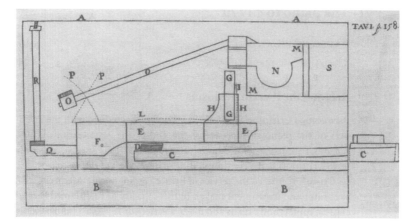

to undergo innumerable modifications, refinements and enlargements over nearly 200 years before it became the sophisticated instrument that we know today. The early piano-actions were extremely light and delicate and the sound very restricted to our ears, but, compared to other keyboard instruments, the first pianos had the advantage of combining sensitivity of touch with relatively substantial tone.

Despite the cleverness and newness of Cristofori's instruments, the 'gravicembalo col piano e forte' (harpsichord with soft and loud) did not arouse much interest in Italy, and the new instrument was further developed in Germany. Here, in the early 1730s, a well-known organ and clavichord maker, Gottfried Silbermann (1683–1753), began to experiment with the new action of the piano. He took Cristofori's design and more or less copied it, gradually adding further sophistications. In 1760 twelve German piano craftsmen went to England, some of them from Silbermann's workshop. One of them, Johannes Zumpe (1726–90), developed a simple piano mechanism which he incorporated into an oblong case, thus producing what was unaccountably called a 'square' piano. These instruments became immensely popular as they were relatively inexpensive to buy and did not take up much room. For the first time, the piano was available as a domestic instrument to the rising middle classes. From 1768, it also began to feature in concert programmes. A Dutch maker in London, Americus Backers (flourished 1763–78), started to make grand pianos around this time. His example was followed by John Broadwood (1732–1812), who

Fig. 3.4. Square piano by Johannes Zumpe and Gabriel Buntebart, London, 1777–8.

started his own business, a firm which is still in existence today. Thus the tradition of English piano making was established, with instruments which are the forerunners of today's pianos. They are quite substantial, rich and full in tone, with pedals to raise all the dampers, and a mechanism (the *una corda*) to shift the keyboard sideways, so that only one string is struck for each note instead of the usual two or three.

Meanwhile in Germany a separate development had taken place. A group of makers had been attempting to make a sort of improved clavichord, without much success. Their work was taken forward by Johann Andreas Stein (1728–92), who is usually credited with inventing a different type of action from those of Cristofori, Silbermann and the English school. This was the 'Prellmechanik', which came to be known as the German or Viennese action. It was simpler and lighter than the English action, producing a clear, silvery tone with very precise damping. Initially these instruments had hand-stops (like those on a harpsichord) rather than pedals, or knee-levers under the keyboard which were pushed up or to one side to raise the dampers. There was also a mechanism, the 'moderator', which inserted a thin piece of felt between the hammers and the strings, producing a beautiful soft tone. Stein's pianos became popular; Mozart met him in 1777, and wrote enthusiastically about his instruments. In the early years of the nineteenth century, pedals were introduced to the Viennese pianos, sometimes as many as five or six: one to raise the dampers (sustaining), one for the keyboard shift (*una corda* – with this the hammer could strike one or two out of the three strings), two for different thicknesses of moderator, and one for a 'bassoon' sound (parchment placed on the string to give a curious buzzing effect) or for 'Turkish music', imitating drums, bells and cymbals! So these instruments were rich in devices for producing different sonorities, particularly in the softer registers. This explains why Schubert employed so many *piano* and *pianissimo* markings in his keyboard music.

Both the English and the Viennese instruments initially had wooden frames, but from about 1800 metal bars began to be used to maintain the increasing tension of the strings, especially in the English instruments. Classical pianos were 'straight-strung', that is the bass strings did not cross over the treble as they do now. The hammers were covered in leather rather than felt (which was first used in about 1825). The range of the instruments increased from five octaves in the 1780s to six and a half in the 1820s.

Fig. 3.5. Mozart's piano, built in 1780 by the Viennese maker Anton Walter.

It was the English action which eventually led to the modern piano action, though an important contribution was made by the French maker Sébastien Erard, who, in 1821, developed the 'double escapement' action permitting rapid repetition of a single note. The Viennese action flourished for about a hundred years, but then fell out of use because, with its delicacy and sensitivity, it could never produce the volume necessary to fill the larger concert halls or compete with the enlarged orchestra. However, this is the action which was known and used exclusively by Mozart and Schubert and many of their contemporaries. Haydn and Beethoven knew both types of piano: Haydn because he visited London in the 1790s; Beethoven because he was sent a piano by Broadwood in 1817. For both composers the exposure to the different instruments had a marked effect on their music. Compare, for example, Haydn's two sonatas in E flat, Hob. XVI Nos. 49 and 52, written within a few years of each other. The first was composed in Vienna, and the second in London. The two clearly imply different sonorities and different techniques, the earlier one needing mostly a light finger-touch, the later requiring a heavier touch with more use of arm weight.

Fig. 3.6. Grand piano by John Broadwood & Sons, London, 1816.

Speaking and feeling

The rapid changes in keyboard instruments in the eighteenth and early nineteenth centuries reflect a change in musical communication which has been described by the conductor and early music specialist Nikolaus Harnoncourt (in his *Baroque Music Today*, 1988):

> Articulation is the technical process in producing speech, the way in which different vowels and consonants are produced... Problems of articulation are especially apparent...in music from about 1600 to 1800 since, as a rule, this music is basically related to speech. The parallels to speech were strongly emphasized by all theorists of the period. Music was often described as 'speech in tones.' To put this in simplified...terms, I like to say that music prior to 1800 speaks, while subsequent music paints. The former must be understood, since anything that is spoken presupposes understanding. The latter affects us by means of moods which need not be understood, because they should be felt.

Harnoncourt's point is illuminated by comparing the slow movement of Mozart's Sonata in B flat K. 570 (1789), say, with the G flat Impromptu by Schubert (1827). Both are serious, introspective pieces, but their emotional content and the effect of the music is very different: it might be said that the Mozart is 'understood' and that the Schubert is 'felt'. In part, this reflects changes in the Viennese piano between the two works. Mozart's piano would have had a clear, relatively dry sound: this admirably suits the precise articulation which is required, even in this slow movement. The knee-lever might be used to raise the dampers occasionally, though not very often, and the moderator might be used in some passages. Schubert's piano was larger, with a richer tone, and with pedals which would have been used frequently: the sustaining pedal certainly, and probably, at different times, all the mechanisms for producing a softer tone. Both pieces have beautiful melodies, but the Mozart proceeds in 'punctuated' statements, while the Schubert is one long line with a wash of harmony underneath it. We may prefer one or the other, but what is interesting is how inextricably linked the music is to the age in which it was written, and to the instrument on which it would have been played.

Playing the music on modern pianos

Nowadays most of us play music from Bach to Bartók and beyond on one instrument, an instrument that was developed at the end of the nineteenth century and which has not changed a great deal since. Its qualities and sound grew out of the music of the second half of the nineteenth century, the height of the Romantic movement and the beginning of twentieth-century Modernism. The social, economic and artistic conditions at that time were very different from those of the Classical period. Without exercising considerable care, it is all too easy for nuances of earlier music to be obscured by the homogeneous and glossy sound of the modern piano. The early pianos had highly individual voices and a fascinating variety of tone and texture, much of which has been lost in the search for the larger and more sustained sound of the concert grand. Also, we no longer have some of the devices which changed the sonority so effectively, such as the moderator or the original *una corda* mechanism. So what can we learn from the early pianos, and how might this affect our manner of playing the rich heritage of the Viennese masters on the modern instrument? Here are some comments and suggestions.

Hand position and fingering

At the beginning of the Classical period keyboard technique was derived from the requirements of the harpsichord and the clavichord. Although there were differences between these instruments, as described above, the instruction books invariably ask for a quiet hand with clear and distinct finger-action. C. P. E. Bach, in his famous *Versuch über die wahre Art das Clavier zu spielen* (translated as *Essay on the True Art of Playing Keyboard Instruments*), first published in 1753, advised:

> In playing, the fingers should be arched and the muscles relaxed. The less these two conditions are satisfied, the more attention must be given to them. Stiffness hampers all movements, above all the constantly required rapid extension and contraction of the hands.

In his *Clavierschule* of 1789 D. G. Türk wrote:

> The fingers must not be held too closely together, but rather a little apart from each other, so that whenever possible, any stretches can be executed nicely and with continuity, without motion of the hands, because playing should be done only with the fingers. For larger skips, however, small movements of the hands and arms are unavoidable.

This emphasis on the quietness and fluidity of the hand continued long after the piano had gained its supremacy over the older instruments, and even when the musical content of the early nineteenth-century keyboard repertoire began to demand more drama and rhetoric in its presentation. Beethoven, according to a pupil, taught that:

> The hands always lie on the keyboard in such a way that the fingers cannot be raised more than necessary, for only in this way is it possible to create *tone* and to learn to *sing*. He detested the staccato style [and] called it 'finger-dancing' or 'manual air-sawing'.

However, the larger instruments and the greater technical demands made by composers, especially the sheer volume required in chordal and octave passages, led inevitably to an increasing use of arm weight and the different forms of staccato. Even so, the numerous books of exercises and studies of the time, and the instruction manuals which proliferated in the nineteenth century, all continue to place great importance on keeping shoulders, arms and wrists relaxed, and on the avoidance of unnecessary movement.

Fingering had been a subject of fascination from the early days of keyboard playing. In the Baroque period the choice of fingering was more closely linked to articulation and phrasing than it is now, when comfort and convenience are foremost in players' minds. An aspect of fingering that was strongly emphasized in the middle of the eighteenth century was the use of the thumb, and especially its turning under in scale and arpeggio passages – which hitherto had not been consistently applied. J. S. Bach had made this an essential part of his technique, and it was firmly advocated by his son C. P. E.:

> The thumbs give the hand not only another digit, but the key to all fingering. This principal finger performs another service in that it keeps the others supple, for they must remain arched as it makes its entry after one or another of them...

The importance of careful consideration of fingering when learning pieces is constantly emphasized. Here is C. P. E. Bach again:

> If (the performer) understands the correct principles of fingering and has not acquired the habit of making unnecessary gestures, he will play the most difficult things in such a manner that the motion of his hands will be barely noticeable; moreover, everything will sound as if it presented no obstacles to him.

And this is Türk:

> It is well known that fingering is an essential...part of keyboard playing. Therefore, the student must work very diligently...to acquire commendable fingering habits, because it is not possible to play in a well-rounded and free-flowing manner when using poor and incorrect fingerings... The most comfortable fingering, or that which requires the least movement of the hands, is generally regarded as being the best.

In these two famous textbooks alone, a total of ninety-seven pages is devoted to the subject of fingering, with numerous examples.

Articulation and pedalling

C. P. E. Bach wrote in his *Essay*:

> In general the briskness of allegros is expressed by detached notes and
> the tenderness of adagios by broad slurred notes... There are many who
> play stickily, as if they had glue between their fingers. Their touch is
> lethargic; they hold notes too long. Others, in an attempt to correct this,
> leave the keys too soon, as if they burned. Both are wrong. Midway
> between these extremes is best.

Because of the emphasis on long legato lines during the nineteenth
century, it is often forgotten that throughout the eighteenth century a non-
legato touch was the norm, and that short or long notes were the exception
(see also Chapter 2 'Notation and Interpretation', p. 21). Staccato was indicated by a dot or a stroke, which often implied an accent as well, while long
notes were marked with a slur or phrase mark. Any unmarked notes were
to be played about half their length, though the actual length would
depend on the context, that is on the mood or 'affect' of the piece. In the
words of C. P. E. Bach:

> Tones which are neither detached, connected, nor fully held are sounded
> for half their value, unless the abbreviation Ten. (hold) is written over
> them, in which case they must be held fully. Crotchets and quavers in
> moderate and slow tempos are usually performed in this semi-detached
> manner. They must not be played weakly, but with fire and a slight
> accentuation.

This approach is different from how we tend to play on the modern piano.
It is generally assumed now that everything will be joined (and often
pedalled) unless there is a definite staccato mark. In earlier music there are
long lines, but these lines are articulated, the space or silence between
phrases being a living part of the meaning and shape – just as someone
who is speaking well will use clear consonants and spaces between words
and sentences. We have become accustomed to using the pedal nearly all
the time on the modern piano, so that without it the tone sounds thin to
our ears. Mozart and Haydn certainly used and enjoyed a sustaining
device, but more as a special effect, in the same way as string players used
vibrato. Beethoven begins to demand more use of the sustaining pedal, but
the modern player should not forget the earlier style, and should take care
not to swamp the music with too much pedal. It is always good to practise
for some time without any pedal and then to add it where it is needed. As
late as 1828 Johann Nepomuk Hummel, a pupil of Mozart, wrote in his
piano method:

> Let the Pupil never employ the Pedals before he can play a piece
> correctly and intelligibly. Indeed, generally speaking, every player should
> indulge in them with the utmost moderation; for it is an erroneous
> supposition that a passage, correctly and beautifully executed without
> pedals, and of which every note is clearly understood, will please the
> hearer less, than a mere confusion of sounds, arising from a series of
> notes clashing one against another.

Dynamics

It is obvious that one of the features of the developing piano was the increase in volume. Hammers got larger, strings thicker and soundboards more resonant in order to achieve this aim. However, even the early pianos had a wide range of dynamics, so in playing Mozart and Haydn on the modern piano one should not be afraid to bring out the contrasts. What should be avoided as far as possible is a thickening of the sound, and a ponderous quality which is alien to the clarity and delicacy of their writing and the instruments they played. With Beethoven and Schubert, the textures are sometimes more dense, and on their larger instruments more weight of sound was possible, but even here care must be taken not to force the tone and to make early nineteenth-century music sound like Liszt or Brahms. In particular, the notes in the left hand must sound clearly and distinctly, even in thick chords. Always listen to the lowest note and balance the other notes with that – or, in short, always listen!

The organ

After the great outpouring of organ music in the Baroque era, especially from J. S. Bach, both composers and organ builders were relatively inactive in the Classical period. Mozart loved to play and improvise on the organ, which he considered 'the king of instruments', but he left little music specifically for it. Similarly, Beethoven played the organ as a young man, but composed no organ music. As the organ was used mainly for church services, much of the solo music played on it would have been improvised to fit the liturgical context. Although some fine organs were built in Europe during the period, with hindsight it seems that the organ world was lying in wait for the upsurge of interest in the instrument in the second half of the nineteenth century. However, there was some demand for chamber organs as domestic instruments in the larger houses, especially in England; and there was a growing interest in mechanical instruments, including the elaborate clocks and barrel organs for which Haydn, Mozart and Beethoven all wrote pieces. Players performing works such as Mozart's great F minor Fantasia on modern church organs should remember that the instruments for which they were written were very small – though they might also like to be reminded of Mozart's complaint that they 'consist solely of little pipes, which sound too high-pitched and too childish for my taste'.

'Play from the soul'

The Classical era was surely the most productive sixty or seventy years of music that the world has seen. Quite apart from the many great symphonies, concertos, string quartets and songs written during the period, there was a profusion of music for the new instrument, the piano. As for the content of the music, it is sometimes thought that true emotion did not really show itself until the flowering of the Romantic age, and that the Classical period was mainly concerned with balance, proportion and symmetry. This is a serious misconception. The Classical musicians were concerned to make beautiful forms, but they were even more interested in the substance of the music and in what the forms were expressing.

By way of conclusion, to emphasize this point, here are some extracts from widely read treatises which have much to say to keyboard players, now as then:

> A musician cannot move others unless he too is moved. He must feel all of the affects that he hopes to arouse in his audience, for the revealing of his own humour will stimulate a like humour in the listener... Play from the soul and not like a trained bird! (C. P. E. Bach, 1753)

> Everything depends on good execution. This saying is confirmed by experience. Many a would-be composer is thrilled with delight...when he hears his music played by good performers who know how to produce the effect in the right place; and how to vary the character as much as it is humanly possible to do so, and who therefore know how to make the whole miserable scribble bearable to the ears of the listeners by means of a good performance. (Leopold Mozart, 1756)

> Whoever performs a composition so that the 'affect' (character, etc.), even in every single passage, is most faithfully expressed and that the tones become at the same time a language of feelings, of this person it is said that he is a good executant. Good execution, therefore, is the most important, but at the same time, the most difficult task of making music. (Türk, 1789)

> Beauty of performance supposes everything nicely rounded off, and accurately suited to any given composition, and to every passage in it; it includes whatever is tasteful, pleasing and ornamental. Expression relates immediately to the feelings and denotes in the player a capacity and facility of displaying by his performance, and urging to the heart of his audience, whatever the composer had addressed to the feelings in his production, and which the performer must feel after him... Expression may be awakened indeed but...it can neither be taught nor acquired; it dwells within the soul itself and must be transfused directly from it into the performance. (Hummel, 1828)

Duncan Druce

Strings

The strings in the Classical period

Today, we often admire Classical music for its poise and balance, but at the time the period must have seemed one of rapid, even turbulent change. In the years around 1800, certain instruments were in the process of substantial development. The piano, clarinet and guitar of 1830, for instance, had departed radically from their mid-eighteenth-century forerunners. The evolution of bowed string instruments was much less startling; but violinists, violists, cellists and double-bass players were still able to make all the changes that the musical development of these momentous years demanded. The strings continued to form the backbone of the orchestra, and the enormous, distinguished repertoire of Classical solo and chamber music for strings shows how successfully the instruments and their players surmounted the challenges of the new style.

Instrumental developments

The most obvious physical development was of the bow. The variety of different designs in the early eighteenth century was replaced by what has ever since been the standard model, introduced in about 1780 by the Parisian maker François Xavier Tourte the younger (1747/8–1835). The 'Tourte' bow incorporated a number of trends in bow design, towards greater length, a wider band of hair and a more weighty point. It was adopted by players of all the string instruments, though not by every double-bass player: outside France, many of them preferred the out-curved Italian-style bow, on account of its greater attack and strength. This bow, favoured by the greatest bass virtuoso of the time, Domenico Dragonetti (1763–1846), was used underhand, like the modern German 'Simandl' bow.

The violin, viola and cello were also subject to a number of alterations. These didn't dramatically change the instruments' outer appearance, but they did have a big effect on the sound. The neck (and with it the playing length of the strings) was lengthened and made slimmer, for ease of playing in the higher positions. It was morticed on to the body of the instrument at an angle, in contrast to the straight neck of the Baroque instrument, which was nailed on. The bridge was more decisively curved, to accommodate greater bow pressure. Inside the instrument, the soundpost was increased in diameter and the bass-bar made longer and thicker.

The effect of all this was to make the instrument able to withstand and respond to greater string tension, and so to produce a stronger tone. This was part of a general trend. During the eighteenth century, Italian violinists had begun to favour very thick strings made of gut, which, together with the brilliant-sounding instruments of such makers as Stradivari and Giuseppe Guarneri, produced a powerful sound. These preferences spread across Europe and even intensified, promoting a new style of playing.

It is not easy to pinpoint when the changes in construction happened – they involved the conversion of older instruments as well as the making of new ones. But in *The Violin: Its Famous Makers and their Imitators* (1875), George Hart quoted an Italian writer, Vincenzo Lancetti, who in 1823 observed: 'About 1800 the brothers Mantegazza [of Milan]...were often entrusted by French and Italian artistes to lengthen the necks of their violins after the Paris fashion'. Nevertheless, the changes didn't happen overnight, and many stringed instruments have even survived into modern times with their original necks.

The Classical string instruments had lost the typically light, bright sound of their Baroque forebears in favour of a more robust tone – which was, however, still a long way from the smoother, blander effect of modern strings. Plain gut was the norm for the top three strings of the violin and the top two of the viola and cello; the lower strings were of gut wound with silver or copper wire. Double-bass strings were all of plain gut until well into the nineteenth century.

Playing the instruments

We are fortunate that during this period of change many works of detailed technical instruction were published; some of these are now available in modern or facsimile editions. With the help of these, together with performance indications in the musical text and written evidence, we can piece together quite a detailed, if tantalizingly incomplete, picture of how string instruments were played in the Classical era.

Fascinatingly, for a player the 'feel' of the correct Classical instrument goes together with and illuminates the printed information. But a player on a modern instrument, too, will find the attempt to approach a true period sound and style immensely rewarding. In particular, to reinstate the wide variety of bow strokes of the time, to understand their direct connection with expression and phrasing, is to bring the music to life in all its detail and inner workings.

Bowing
Sustained notes

In his violin method of 1756, Leopold Mozart, following the example of Giuseppe Tartini, prescribes as his basic bow-management exercise a long note with gradual crescendo and diminuendo:

p ——<*f* >—— *p*

He also gives some other patterns:

f >—— *p* , *p* ——<*f* or *p* ——<*f* >—— *p* ——<*f* >—— *p*

But only after these does he suggest practising long bow-strokes at an even dynamic level. This order of priority shows the eighteenth century's concern with the details of phrasing, with inflecting the sound so that the music has the same variety of stress and volume as a well-delivered poetic recitation. We can guess that Leopold's basic bowing shape is implied in this solo entry from the slow movement of a concerto by his son:

Ex. 4.1.
W. A. Mozart, Violin Concerto in B flat major K. 207, 1773: second movement, Adagio, bb. 30–34.

Leopold Mozart's treatise was published in several editions until after the turn of the century. But by 1803, when Pierre Baillot, Rudolphe Kreutzer and Pierre Rode produced the 'official' *Méthode de violon* for the new Paris Conservatoire, the perspective had altered. The series of scales in every key which form the basic elementary exercises 'must be played with the notes sustained strongly from one end of the bow to the other…the tempo must, in general, be very slow'. We can imagine the broad, sustained bowing advocated by the Paris violinists being applied in the following passage:

Ex. 4.2. Beethoven, Violin Concerto in D major Op. 61, 1806: second movement, Larghetto, solo violin, bb. 45–50.

Rapid passages

The smooth joining of bow strokes in *adagio* or cantabile playing seems to have been a universal aim throughout the Classical period (and since). What may surprise a modern player is the insistence that bow speed should be varied according to the tempo and character of the music. In J. F. Reichardt's *Ueber die Pflichten des Ripien-Violinisten* (1776, Essay on the Duties of the Orchestral Violinist) we read: 'In allegro, a brisk bow for staccato, and a fast stroke at the start of a bow is absolutely essential'.

Clearly, in the eighteenth century a brisk *allegro* bowing went together with a shortening of many notes (particularly repeated notes or leaps). Leopold Mozart describes how this shortening is achieved by lifting the bow from the string, but this doesn't imply a bounced bowing. It applies rather to notes long enough for a stroke starting on the string to be lifted, as with the repeated quavers in Ex. 4.3:

For shorter notes, such as semiquavers in *allegro*, a short stroke near the middle of a 'pike-head' or 'swan-bill head' bow (of the type illustrated by Leopold, Fig. 4.1) produces a natural articulation, softer than, and not as short as, a modern *spiccato* bowing. This isn't easy to achieve precisely with a modern bow, but by holding the stick a few centimetres from the nut and playing a short *détaché* stroke near the middle it's possible to make a good approximation.

Ex. 4.3.
W. A. Mozart, Violin Concerto in A major K. 219, 1775: first movement, Allegro aperto, solo violin, bb. 74–8.

Fig. 4.1. L. Mozart, *Versuch einer gründlichen Violinschule* (1756): illustration showing 'swan-bill head' bow and early-Classical playing position.

Fig. 4.1. L. Mozart, *Versuch einer gründlichen Violinschule* (1756): illustration showing 'swan-bill head' bow and early-Classical playing position.

Even before the Tourte bow had become fully established, the 'hatchet-headed' bows of the later eighteenth century had opened up new possibilities: their design, with its tighter bow-hair, allowed the bow to bounce more readily. Between 1780 and 1800 this springing bow stroke became very popular; it was associated especially with the German violinist Wilhelm Cramer (1746–99), and music such as in Ex. 4.4 seems designed to exploit it:

Ex. 4.4. J. Haydn, Quartet in D major Op. 64 No. 5, 'Lark', 1790: fourth movement, Vivace, violin I, bb. 1–8.

This bowing is very different from the type described in the Paris Conservatoire method of 1803: 'In the Allegro, the bow stroke will be shorter, beginning about three-quarters of the way along the bow, and with no separation between the notes'. This is the broad, grand style of playing associated with Giovanni Battista Viotti, the teacher of Rode, one of the authors of the method; it will be familiar to student violinists who have attempted the Kreutzer studies (for example, Nos. 2, 3 and 8). Rode's playing profoundly influenced Louis Spohr (1784–1859), who became a lifelong and immensely influential promoter of broad, on-the-string bowing. The move towards a more brilliant, varied style, under the influence of Paganini, had only just begun by the end of the Classical period.

For longer note values in a lively movement, where Leopold Mozart would have lifted the bow, later players rested it on the string between notes. This could produce a sharp *martelé* (literally a 'hammered' stroke) at the point (as in the sixth Kreutzer study). Or the player could use a similar technique to make a much broader stroke: 'In an Allegro moderato or Moderato assai,...the *détaché* must be given as much length of bow as possible, up to about a half-bow, so that the sounds are resonant [*rondes*] and the string vibrates to its full extent' (Paris *Méthode*). These on-the-string detached bowings have largely gone out of fashion in the last hundred years, but the off-the-string style that we use instead doesn't sound the same: it can give a lively, flexible impression, but it lacks the rhythmic control and panache that Viotti or Spohr would have achieved.

Cellists didn't attempt a forceful *martelé* at the point. The methods of Jean-Louis Duport, Friedrich Dotzauer and Bernhard Heinrich Romberg all recommend that strong detached passages should be played in the middle of the bow, reserving the point for more delicate effects.

Up-bow or down-bow?

> As regards bowing there are no definite rules for determining whether one should begin with a down-bow or up-bow. (Tartini, *c*.1750)

> ...one endeavours to take the first note of each bar with a down stroke, and this even if two down strokes should follow each other... To this rule only the quickest tempo necessitates an exception being made. (L. Mozart, 1756)

At first sight these statements are contradictory. But from Tartini we learn that Italian virtuosos could allow themselves considerable freedom in bowing; and there's the implication that correct phrasing and accentuation should stem from the player's mind, and be achievable independently of the mechanics of instrumental technique. On the other hand, Leopold Mozart proposes a series of rules that enable a group of string players to achieve unanimity of phrasing. Mozart's recommendations, which in 1756 already had a long history, also reflect eighteenth-century composers' thoughts on musical metres in relation to stress-patterns: one accent per bar in 2/4, ¢, 3/4 and 6/8; two per bar in c and 12/8. In this context it's entirely logical to use the natural weight of the down-bow to bring out the

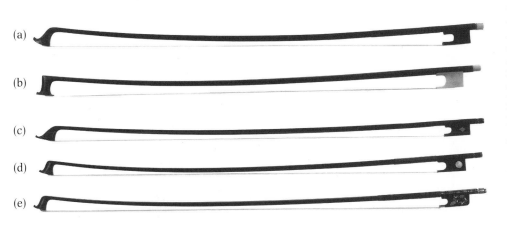

Fig. 4.2. Violin bows, by (a) Nicolas Pierre Tourte (Tourte *père*) *c*.1760; (b) Edward Dodd *c*.1775; (c) John Dodd *c*.1780; (d) John Dodd *c*.1800; (e) anon. (German) *c*.1820. All five bows have concave sticks, generally adopted by the later eighteenth century. (a) and (c) have modified 'pike heads', made higher to accommodate the inward curve; (b) has a heavier 'battle-axe head', while (d) and (e) show the development of the modern 'hatchet head'.

(a)
(b)
(c)
(d)
(e)

underlying rhythmic basis, and to use up-bows for the lifted upbeats that are recommended for all but the slowest, most sostenuto pieces. Exx. 4.5, 4.6 and 4.7 show how the 'rule of down-bow' might apply in some familiar pieces:

Ex. 4.5. Beethoven, Violin Sonata in D major Op. 12 No. 1, 1797–8: third movement, Allegro, bb. 9–13.

Ex. 4.6. W. A. Mozart, Violin Sonata in B flat major K. 454, 1784: first movement, Largo – Allegro, bb. 19–20.

Ex. 4.7. W. A. Mozart, String Quartet in D major K. 575, 1789: second movement, Andante, cello, bb. 42–7. When a slur lasts for a whole bar, the player must choose which bar takes the greater stress, and so needs the down-bow.

Dotted notes and syncopations

The Baroque manner of playing dotted rhythms with separate strokes

 *etc.*

gradually gave way to the 'hooked-in' style

 etc.

This change occurred with the development of the bow, more weight at the point making lifted strokes less natural. Leopold Mozart gives examples of both sorts of bowing, depending on the smoothness of the music, though by the end of the Classical period 'hooked' bowing had become standard. But another bowing for fast, uneven notes seems to have appeared in about 1800: this entailed playing at the point with separate bows, the longer note taken up-bow. Two famous pieces implying this technique are the finales of Beethoven's 'Kreutzer' Sonata for violin and piano and Schubert's 'Death and the Maiden' String Quartet:

Ex. 4.8. F. Schubert, String Quartet in D minor D. 810, 'Death and the Maiden', 1824: fourth movement, Presto, violin I, bb. 1–8.

The most common purpose of syncopated rhythms during the Classical period was to convey agitation or unease:

Ex. 4.9. W. A. Mozart, Piano Concerto in D minor K. 466, 1785: first movement, Allegro, violin I, bb. 1–5.

Today, we commonly hear such syncopations emphasized with an accent at the beginning of each note. But there's evidence that at the time, and into the nineteenth century, a different approach was used. Baillot, in his *L'art du violon* of 1835, gives the most complete description: unless a displaced accent demands that the syncopation be given an initial *sforzando*, or a serene character suggests performance without accentuation, the player should 'swell the note and speed up the bow till the end of the note, but gently' – hence taking care to start the next note quietly. The Classical repertoire is full of passages whose effect is enhanced by this inflected interpretation of syncopations:

Ex. 4.10. Beethoven, Violin Sonata in C minor Op. 30 No. 2, 1801–2: first movement, Allegro con brio, bb. 62–4.

Slurs

Eighteenth-century slurs are indications of bowing patterns, of course, but they are primarily pointers to phrasing and character.

> Now if in a musical composition two, three, four and even more notes be bound together by the half circle, so that one recognises therefrom that the composer wishes the notes not to be separated but to be played singingly in one slur, the first of such united notes must be somewhat more strongly stressed, but the remainder slurred on to it quite smoothly and more and more quietly. (L. Mozart)

This approach to slurring is essential for a stylish interpretation of late eighteenth-century music; it goes together with the idea that longer notes starting on the main beats of the bar (in the faster tempos) are rarely sustained at full volume, and are often shortened. But it's worth noting that Leopold Mozart writes of a gradual diminuendo – what he clearly doesn't want is a sharp attack at the start of the first slurred note.

In his later music, W. A. Mozart often asks for whole passages to be played legato, by means of a continuous pattern of slurs:

This reflects a growing fondness for a smoother style of playing. The slurring pattern does still imply something of the eighteenth-century diminuendo manner, more decisively as the slurs become shorter. But it would surely be a mistake to exaggerate the stresses at the start of each bar: the overall legato line is equally important. Beethoven, too, used continuous slurring patterns to indicate a legato style, but from quite early in his career he also wrote some very long slurs in his string music – often too long, one imagines, to be attempted in a single bow (Exx. 4.12 and 4.13).

Ex. 4.11. W. A. Mozart, Clarinet Quintet in A major K. 581, 1789: first movement, Allegro, violin I, bb. 1–7.

Ex. 4.12. Beethoven, String Quartet in F major Op. 18 No. 1, 1798–1800: fourth movement, Allegro, violin I, bb. 193–9.

Ex. 4.13. Beethoven, String Quartet in F major Op. 59 No. 1, 1806: third movement, Adagio molto e mesto, cello, bb. 72–5.

I feel sure that this is Beethoven's very clear way of showing that he wants a purely legato delivery, without any conventional strong-beat stresses, and with bow-changes made as unobtrusively as possible.

In the Classical period, the tenuto sign (–) was not in general use, but instead we often meet phrases marked with slurs and dots (Ex. 4.14). The Italian writer Francesco Galeazzi, in his *Elementi teorico-pratici di musica* (1791), describes exactly how to play this:

> *Note-portate*, so-called, are those [notes] which are neither separate nor slurred, but almost dragged. They are all played in one stroke without lifting the bow from the string but each note is given a slight articulation with the bow which is not done in slurring.

Ex. 4.14. Beethoven, String Quartet in G major Op. 18 No. 2, 1798–1800: second movement, Adagio cantabile, bb. 81–5.

The final words of this quotation should caution us against a common present-day practice, of slightly articulating the individual notes within a slur; in other words, introducing *portato* as a habit in places where it's not indicated.

When slurs and dots are combined at a faster speed, the intended bow stroke is an on-the-string staccato, each note like a tiny *martelé* stroke:

Ex. 4.15. W. A. Mozart, String Quartet in D major K. 575: first movement, Allegretto, violin I, bb. 66–7.

Ex. 4.16. F. Schubert, Piano Quintet in A major D. 667, 'The Trout', 1819: second movement, Andante, violin, bb. 44–5.

It's known that the finest string players of the period, Spohr for instance, were able to execute this bowing at very high speed, and to brilliant effect.

Chords

During the Classical period, string players moved from the Baroque style of arpeggiating chords and only sustaining a single note (usually the top one), towards the modern 'two-by-two' technique (described by Spohr in his *Violinschule* of 1832) of splitting a chord to leave two notes sustained on the upper strings. But most chords in the Beethoven sonatas, for example, are short, and should be played with a quick arpeggiation, starting at the heel of the bow. Where more sustained chords occur there's scope for alternatives. The opening of Mozart's Sonata K. 454 sounds best if only the top note is held:

Ex. 4.17. W. A. Mozart, Violin Sonata in B flat major K. 454: first movement, Largo – Allegro, bb. 1–3.

But the start of Beethoven's Op. 12 No. 1 benefits from the extra resonance given by sustaining the upper two notes:

Ex. 4.18. Beethoven, Violin Sonata in D major Op. 12 No. 1: first movement, Allegro con brio, bb. 1–3.

Vibrato

Vibrato was well known in the eighteenth century, usually classed as an ornament, and recommended by Geminiani, Tartini and Leopold Mozart. Geminiani suggests that it may be employed on longer notes, while Mozart castigates those 'who tremble consistently on each note as if they had the palsy'. Tartini recommends its use on long final notes, but he also suggests vibrato at an increasing speed to accompany a crescendo on a sustained note. Both Tartini and Mozart (who bases his discussion on Tartini's) ask for a regular vibration that follows the rhythm of the music, even when at an *adagio* tempo this means a rate which seems extraordinary to us – one vibration per crotchet beat.

The use of vibrato actually declined in the early nineteenth century. Dotzauer, in his *Violoncellschule* (1832), expresses the general view that it should be used only rarely, on long notes, and that it's more important for the cellist to cultivate the finest tone without vibrato. Spohr and Baillot (1835) give detailed examples of how and where it should be used – Spohr's bar-by-bar instructions on the interpretation of his Ninth Concerto and Rode's Seventh include details of vibrato, with signs to indicate the speed of vibration:

Ex. 4.19. L. Spohr, Violin Concerto No. 9 in D minor Op. 55, 1820: first movement, Allegro, bb. 57–64, showing the composer's annotations as printed in *Violinschule* (1832).

It may be difficult for a modern string player to abandon continuous vibrato, but a more sparing, selective use of it will certainly help to give varied expression to the music. And continuous vibrato as an aid to sostenuto tone-production is not suitable on those occasions, particularly in eighteenth-century music, where legato bowing is to be avoided:

Ex. 4.20. W. A. Mozart, String Quintet in C minor K. 406, 1788: first movement, Allegro, violin I, bb. 1–5. Here, the loudest parts of the first three notes should be near the start; if vibrato is used at all, it should decline with the bow speed towards the end of each note. Bar 3 could be sustained with vibrato, and bar 4 played as a gradual diminuendo, with vibrato on the *eb″* only.

Fig. 4.3. F. Dotzauer, *Violoncellschule* (1832): illustration showing cello playing position. Note the slightly tilted playing position, with the cello resting on the right calf, and the 'square-on' left-hand position, introduced by Duport; earlier cellists had the fingers pointing downwards.

Fingering

Violinists and violists of the Classical period were more ready to use the 'unpopular' 2nd and 4th positions than their nineteenth-century successors. Before 1800, players didn't all adopt the firm chin-braced hold, and changing position was a complex procedure, involving steadying the instrument with the left thumb: so they were keen to find the best position to accommodate a complete phrase or passage. But Baillot, in 1835, describes a changing approach during the previous decades, distinguishing between Viotti's preference for staying in one position and crossing from one string to another and the younger violinist Rode's liking for the unified tone-colour of a single string, needing many more position changes. As for cello fingering, it was only during this period that the standard patterns used today were codified, notably by Duport in his *Essai sur le doigté du violoncelle* (1806). Among writers on the cello, there's also an awareness of the contrast between the colourful effect of moving from string to string and the beautiful uniformity of staying on the same string.

In deciding whether to change position or cross strings, then, the player should take into account the date of the composition and the character of the music. Sometimes composers made it easy to decide, by writing music that lies obviously in a particular position:

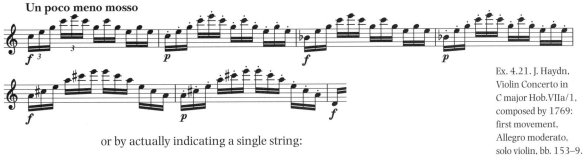

Ex. 4.21. J. Haydn, Violin Concerto in C major Hob.VIIa/1, composed by 1769: first movement, Allegro moderato, solo violin, bb. 153–9.

or by actually indicating a single string:

Ex. 4.22. J. Haydn, String Quartet in A major Op. 20 No. 6, 1772: third movement, Menuetto and Trio (Allegretto), violin I, bb. 21–8.

In the later eighteenth century, writers generally suggest avoiding the open strings: 'He who plays a solo does well if he allows the open strings to be heard but rarely or not at all'. (L. Mozart)

Mozart was also scathing about the use of harmonics; nor did he allow a trill on an open string. But fourth-finger trills were never forbidden, and indeed form an important part of the Classical violinist and violist's technique (Kreutzer's sixteenth study provides excellent practice material!). In the music of the early nineteenth century, the open strings and harmonics are used quite freely – perhaps because the fashion for minimal vibrato means that they sound less obtrusive.

Greater dominance of legato playing in later Classical music had important implications for left-hand technique. In his 1751 *The Art of Playing on the Violin*, Geminiani had recommended a 'clean' finger technique, with no hint of any sliding between notes; but glissandos were certainly not unknown in the later eighteenth century. However, sliding from one note to another was generally a quaint, colourful effect, rather than a serious expressive device:

Ex. 4.23. J. Haydn, String Quartet in E flat major Op. 64 No. 6, 1790: third movement, Menuet and Trio (Allegretto), violin I, bb. 37–42.

Early nineteenth-century fingering suggests a dramatically different picture. Baillot, for instance, gives detailed instructions for making 'ports de voix' (portamenti), asking for a crescendo to coincide with upward slides (Ex. 4.24). Downward slides would, conversely, be accompanied by a diminuendo. Baillot's upward portamenti (and also those recommended by Spohr) are to be made with the finger playing the starting note. Similar

Ex. 4.24. G. B. Viotti, Violin Concerto No. 18 in E minor (*c.*1790–93): first movement, bb. 74–85, as cited in P. Baillot, *L'art du violon* (1835).

instructions are given in the cello methods; the main difference, stemming from the different finger patterns on the larger instrument, is the greater liking for upward slides using the same finger at the start and finish.

There is, perhaps, only limited opportunity for portamenti in the earlier Classical repertoire. But Ex. 4.25 shows where one might be introduced to good effect:

Ex. 4.25. Beethoven, Violin Sonata in E flat major Op. 12 No. 3, 1797–8: second movement, Adagio con molto espressione, bb. 8–10.

By the time of Schubert, however, composers were writing string music that lends itself naturally to the introduction of expressive portamenti:

Ex. 4.26. F. Schubert, Violin Sonata in A major D. 574, 1817: first movement, Allegro moderato, bb. 5–10.

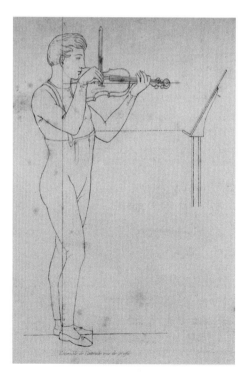

Fig. 4.4. P. Baillot, *L'art du violon*: illustration showing late-Classical playing position.

Double bass

Even today the double bass is a less standardized instrument than the other strings. In the years around 1800 its shape and size, the design of the bow, the tuning and the fingering technique were all subject to wide variation. In his 1752 flute method, the German writer Quantz had described a four-string bass, with the usual modern tunings as customary. He also recommended frets, to produce a clearer sound. The later eighteenth century saw the double bass rise to popularity as a solo instrument. The centre of this trend was Austria, where soloists commonly used a five-string instrument,

tuned

Meanwhile in England, France and Italy, three-stringed basses were usual, preferred for their greater resonance and evenness of response.

These were tuned   or, in France

The tuning in 5ths made it necessary to change position continually, while three-string players often had to transpose the bass lines of orchestral music up an octave. The bass virtuoso Dragonetti favoured the three-string instrument. Contemporary accounts of his playing suggest he sometimes used extended fingering, with the thumb and each finger playing a successive semitone, as described by Francesco Caffi, Dragonetti's first biographer. Far more usual, however, was the technique in which successive semitones were fingered 1, 2, 4 or 1, 3, 4.

Harp

During the eighteenth century the pedal harp, on which the pitch of a single row of strings could be altered chromatically, gradually took the place of the double and triple harps of the Baroque period. It was in Paris, during the second part of the century, that interest in the harp was most intense, and where the main developments in its design and mechanism took place. The eighteenth-century pedal harp was a single-action instrument. With all the strings in their lower position it would play in E flat major; with adjustment of the pedals, the instrument could modulate to six further major keys and five minor ones. It was for such an instrument that Mozart wrote his Concerto for flute and harp, and Krumpholtz, Dussek and Spohr (who were all married to harpists) composed their harp music.

In 1810 Sébastien Erard patented his double-action harp, the basis of harp design ever since. Not only did the new mechanism allow the harp to be tuned in any major or minor key, but the sound quality was more even. The modern harp has since developed more resonance and is more heavily strung. Like a present-day pianist playing Classical music, a harpist needs to develop a precise, even finger-technique in order to perform scale passages, trills and other figuration.

Guitar

After 1750 the essentially alto-register five-course Baroque guitar began to be viewed in a different light, with bass octaves and, sometimes, extra strings added to the lower courses. Six-course guitar music first appeared in Spain in 1780, and double-strung guitars were popular there until the

end of the Classical period. Meanwhile, the single-strung instrument –
prototype of the modern 'classical' guitar – had developed elsewhere in
Europe; surviving examples from the 1780s were made in Italy, France
and Vienna. The turn towards single stringing shows a decisive move to
punteado (plucked) as opposed to *rasgueado* (strummed) playing; *rasgueado* is
undoubtedly more effective on a double-strung instrument, producing a
bright, jangling sound, whereas single stringing, at higher tension, allows
the player to project melodic lines with more force and expression. By the
turn of the century, makers of single-strung guitars had made changes,
including fan-strutting on the underside of the table, to increase the instrument's resonance. Even so, the guitar of around 1800 had a smaller body
than the modern instrument, and a lighter tone. When performing
Classical pieces on a modern guitar, therefore, players should take care not
to play low-register passages too heavily. The increased string-stop
(distance between the frets) since his time means that some passages in the
work of Fernando Sor, for example, are now quite difficult to stretch. Sor's
Méthode pour la guitare, published in 1830, suggests that by the end of the
Classical period many of the essentials of modern technique had become
established, although use of the fingernails was not yet standard practice.

Colin Lawson

Wind Instruments

Wind playing in the Classical period

There are some very important lessons to be learnt from the history of woodwind and brass performance during the Classical period. As at any time in musical history, the finest soloists were individual personalities with a great deal to communicate about the music. Finding the right character for a piece or movement was one of their priorities, and this affected their choice of tempo, dynamics and tonguing. Most musicians agreed that the principal aim of performers should be to move their audience, and that this was more important than merely having lots of technique. Above all, music was widely compared with speech, so that small-scale slurs and phrasing were paid a lot of attention, just like words in a sentence. Everyone agreed that wind players should try to imitate really good singers, and this is still very good advice. It means not just shaping melodic lines but paying attention to all the detail in the phrasing. This is just like a singer taking great care with both vowels and consonants in the text of a song or operatic aria.

The Classical period was a very exciting time in the development of orchestral wind instruments. When Haydn wrote his first symphony, in 1759, the normal wind section was made up of just two oboes and two horns, with one or two bassoons doubling the cellos. By the time of Schubert's death in 1828, pairs of flutes, oboes, clarinets and bassoons were firmly established in the orchestra, together with a brass section often including three trombones as well as two or four horns and a pair of trumpets. Related family members such as the piccolo and contrabassoon were also beginning to make occasional appearances, for example in Beethoven's Fifth Symphony. Other visitors to the wind section included the basset horn, an extended tenor clarinet beloved of Mozart: two of them play a prominent role in his Requiem. A pair of cors anglais appears in Haydn's Symphony No. 22 ('The Philosopher') of 1764, but the instrument was largely confined to small-scale pieces before its use by Berlioz in the 1830s.

Composers began to make enormous demands on their principal players: Beethoven's symphonies in particular contain some very challenging wind parts. Increasing musical difficulties were reflected in the changing designs of the woodwinds, which gradually acquired more keywork during the early nineteenth century. This was also the period when valves were invented and added to brass instruments – though Beethoven and Schubert both wrote for natural instruments, without valves. The valves certainly made a greater range of notes more secure, but they also changed the character of the sound.

This golden age attracted many leading composers to write concertos for virtually all the orchestral wind instruments. Of course Mozart was the most important, but many others also composed solo music. We can never know how Mozart's favourite players actually sounded, but we can be certain that there was a great deal of character in their music making. The need to move an audience is nowadays often forgotten – even though teachers today sometimes still complain that their pupils can play fast passage-work but don't think enough about the music itself. This very same complaint was expressed 250 years ago by the celebrated flautist and writer Johann Joachim Quantz, who was keen to train musicians who were both skilled and intelligent!

When the Paris Conservatoire opened in 1795, after the French Revolution, it published instruction books for most instruments. Like Quantz's *Versuch einer Anweisung die Flöte traversiere zu spielen* (1752, translated as *On Playing the Flute*), the wind tutors emphasized that it was not sufficient merely to read the notes and play the music: flair and imagination were essential. It was important to characterize the music, and not feel restricted by the mere notes on the page. One member of the Conservatoire staff, the clarinettist Xavier Lefèvre, remarked that wind instruments could soon sound monotonous without variety of sound and articulation, admitting that the coldness of tone sometimes attributed to his own instrument was in fact the responsibility of the performer. Most importantly, all writers agreed that a knowledge of harmony was essential for any player of a melody instrument. It was (and remains) important to study one's accompaniments (especially piano parts).

In an age before recordings there was certainly much more variety of styles in solo wind playing. There was also much less standardization of instrument design among European manufacturers than we have become used to, although it comes as no surprise to learn that Vienna was one of the most important centres. One writer remarked in 1811 that players and their wind instruments varied so much from one to the next that there

Fig. 5.1. Wind band of the Prince of Oettingen-Wallerstein, 1791.

could be no set fingerings: it was the responsibility of each player to discover what would work best. There's still room for a little more of this type of creative fingering among performers, even with today's modern instruments. It was during the twentieth century that class teaching in conservatories, the development of recording, and easy communication all combined to encourage a degree of standardization in wind instrument performance and manufacture which is quite different from the conditions in which Mozart and Beethoven worked.

The instruments

What musical hints can be learnt from the wind instruments of the period themselves? There's now much more opportunity to sample the sound of originals and copies, both in the concert hall and on record. By comparison with their modern equivalents, all the instruments sound leaner and less smooth and even in tone. Just as Mozart wrote operatic roles for specific singers, so his concertos were tailored to particular instruments and their players. Mozart never complained about the limitations of any instrument, but simply wrote perfect music for what was available. It's too easy (and misguided) to assume nowadays that wind instruments have simply improved, and that old models are out of date and of no interest. Our modern versions of all the wind and brass were fully established at a time nearer to the middle of the nineteenth century, when a more Romantic and continuous musical style was in evidence. In the lifetimes of Haydn, Mozart, Beethoven and Schubert, the upper woodwinds continued to be manufactured in boxwood, a much lighter material than today's usual blackwoods. It is worth remembering that they were each quite delicate in sound. Flutes, oboes, clarinets and bassoons all had much less keywork   than we are used to. When extra mechanism was added at the beginning of the nineteenth century, it was initially to make trills easier to play, and later to make the instruments more versatile technically and also more powerful. On instruments such as the four-keyed flute or two-keyed oboe, many of the notes had to be played using cross-fingerings (covering one or more notes below an open hole, as for many notes on the recorder), and the unevenness of tone from one note to the next was exploited by composers in various ways.

Double and single reeds varied considerably in design from those in use today. The earliest surviving oboe reeds date from around 1770; reeds gradually became more refined until achieving their modern shape in the

Fig. 5.2. Eight-keyed rosewood flute by Tebaldo Monzani, 1812.

Fig. 5.3. Two- and
eight-keyed oboes,
with reed, after
August Grenzer,
*c.*1760 and
H. Grenzer, *c.*1810.

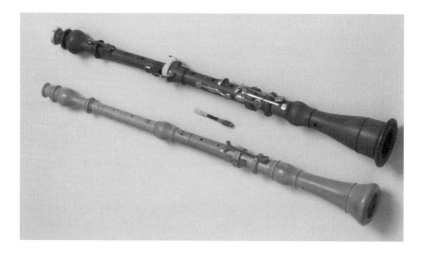

middle of the nineteenth century. However, it would be a mistake to imagine that early reeds encouraged coarseness of sound; rather their designs were well matched to the character of the instruments. Furthermore, differing shapes of reed have contributed to differences in tone quality between French and German oboes since the seventeenth century, the French sound tending to delicacy, the German to warm robustness. Clarinet mouthpieces usually had tapered profiles carrying narrow, short reeds. The clarinet tone-quality of the time of Mozart and Beethoven is probably closest, in terms of present-day schools of playing, to the modern German sound; but it was undoubtedly far less standardized than is the case today. There are some excellent photographs of historical oboe and bassoon reeds and clarinet reeds and mouthpieces illustrating the articles on these instruments in *The New Grove Dictionary of Music and Musicians.*

  The natural horn was used by all the great composers of the period. Players of the instrument all had as their primary aim consistency of tone. This was a challenge given that melodic lines frequently included 'open' notes and 'stopped' notes; the latter had to be obtained by inserting the hand into the bell, which produced a more rasping sound quality. Certainly these instruments did not produce the degree of smoothness available on today's wider-bore, valved horns. The horn's similarity to the human voice was widely remarked upon, as was its ability to imitate feelings of love, sadness and horror. Mozart's concertos show a remarkable grasp of the capabilities of the natural horn, and later in the music of Weber it became a truly Romantic voice.

Although the natural trumpet remained physically the same as in the Baroque period, the Baroque use of the extreme high register gradually

Ex. 5.1. Harmonic
series on C. Notes in
black are out of tune
in equal tempera-
ment. Horns could
obtain intervening
notes by stopping.

Fig. 5.4. Horn with tuning slide and decorated bell by Raoux, Paris, 1818.

declined; orchestral parts instead made different demands, including soft held notes. The concertos by Haydn and Hummel were written for a newly invented (and relatively short-lived) keyed trumpet, which could produce a full chromatic range. Significantly, it had a softer sound than the natural trumpet, perhaps more similar to that of the modern flugelhorn. The trombone was also relatively gentle in sound, at least until the influence of military music (in the wake of the French Revolution) began to coarsen its tone. Schubert used the instrument to great effect, for example including a trio of trombones in his 'Great C major' Symphony.

How did performances of the time actually sound? We can never really be certain, since recording was still some way in the future. But it's perhaps rather too easy to assume that there has been a continuous improvement over the past 200 years in all aspects of playing; it's probably more accurate to assume that priorities have changed. Without doubt, tuning was a preoccupation with most players and writers. In 1752 Quantz noted that cold temperatures could be a difficulty for the flute player, and warned that

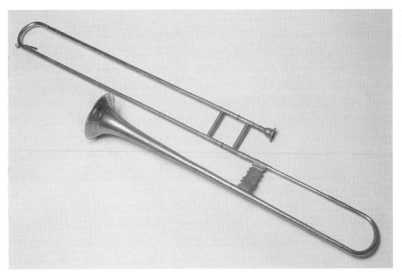

Fig. 5.5. Tenor trombone after J. J. Schmied, Nuremberg, c.1778.

players should always listen to their intonation with great care. In 1791 the Leipzig flautist Johann George Tromlitz suggested that a good flute teacher should play scales with pupils, so that they could hear each interval accurately.

Tone quality

It has always been difficult to explain in words such matters as musicianship and tone quality, but descriptions of players in Mozart's circle of friends offer much food for thought and inspiration. When Mozart's Serenade for thirteen instruments K. 361 received its first known performance, in 1784, the clarinettist Anton Stadler was praised by one critic in the following glowing terms:

> I have never heard the like of what you contrived with your instrument. Never would I have thought that a clarinet could be capable of imitating the human voice as it was imitated by you. Indeed your instrument has so soft and lovely a tone that no one with a heart can resist it.

This reference to the voice is important evidence not just for clarinettists but for all wind players. In the 1790s Stadler was commissioned to draw up plans for the establishment of a music school in Hungary, and he insisted that every student should learn the basic principles of singing, whatever the quality of an individual's voice. (He also reckoned that anyone wishing to understand music should know 'the whole of worldly wisdom', as well as mathematics, poetry, public speaking, art and many languages!) Tromlitz said something quite similar:

> Because not all persons are fond of the same kind of tone, but differ amongst themselves in this matter, it is therefore impossible to establish a tone quality that can be recognized as beautiful by everyone. This goes to show that tone is a matter of taste. I think that the only model on which an instrumentalist should form his tone is the human voice, and as far as I am concerned a human voice that is beautiful is one that is bright, full and resonant, of masculine strength, but not shrieking; soft, not hollow; in short, for me a beautiful voice is full of timbre, rounded, singing, soft and flexible.

It can easily happen that long notes seem more alive and vibrant in singing than in wind playing. But these notes were certainly shaped by instrumentalists throughout the Classical period and beyond. For example, there is overwhelming evidence that the *messa di voce* (or swell <>) continued to be applied to long notes. It was specifically mentioned by the English historian Charles Burney in his account of the celebrated oboist Carlo Besozzi. This swell effect can be an important element in maintaining the character of the music during longer note-values. The very sharp attack with which modern wind players often begin notes is a decidedly non-vocal effect which has no clear historical precedent.

On the other hand, it is clear that vibrato was not used consistently throughout a movement or piece, as often happens today. Evidence of a breath vibrato is patchy, and it was only ever used as an occasional ornament; no tutors for the reed instruments mention it at all. Having admired

Fig. 5.6. Five-keyed clarinet in B flat by Moussetter, Paris, *c*.1800.

the oboist Johann Christian Fischer's style in 1765, Mozart criticized him severely in 1787, writing: 'His tone is entirely nasal, and his held notes like the tremulant on the organ'. As an exception to prove the rule, one Viennese writer in 1796 suggested that vibrato could 'be produced on no other instrument with such expressiveness and vigour as on the horn', and that the horn's richness of effect existed 'because of the roundness and fullness of its tone and because of its vibrato'. The earliest reference to clarinet vibrato appears in 1832, as a specific instruction in Glinka's *Trio pathétique*. By this time Glinka clearly assumed that vibrato could readily be produced if required, and its presence in such an Italianate and vocal piece is perhaps not altogether surprising. But the balance of evidence is that one should be careful not to use too much continuous vibrato in the Classical repertoire.

Articulation

Much modern wind playing aims to achieve a smooth legato; but in the Classical period the approach was much more subtle and complex. Quantz, who described music as 'nothing but an artificial language', listed a vast range of tongue strokes to match the various bow strokes used by violinists. The appropriate tonguing for any note depended chiefly on the speed and character of the movement, and whether the note in question was on the main beat of the bar or a weak beat. Tongue strokes, like consonants in words, were expected to vary widely in emphasis and definition. Classical composers give us a great deal of expressive information by way of small-scale slurs over just two or three notes. Mozart's father, Leopold, and other writers, recommended that within a slur the first note should be stressed rather strongly, with the remaining notes slurred on to it quite smoothly with a gradual diminuendo. This advice continued to apply to pairs of notes, as late as the music of Brahms. If we are to make use of all this detail, we need to play from editions which do not alter or corrupt the composer's original phrasing.

In passage-work without phrase marks, for example in Mozart concertos, the performer was expected to supply articulation. One favourite pattern in the Classical period, though not the Baroque, was two slurred, two tongued, in alternation. Longer note-values without slurs were detached as a matter of course.

One reason why a wind player needed such a good knowledge of harmony was that there was an important general rule that dissonances should be emphasized and leaned on, and then consonances played more quietly. The way a melody was played was determined by its shape and chromatic colouring, the relative importance of notes within the bar, and the underlying harmony. In short, it was expected that a performer would gather a great deal of information about how to play from the rhythm, melodic intervals, phrasing and harmony written in the score, and would then take care to give the music the appropriate character. It's worth noting what Quantz considered poor execution: faulty intonation, a forced tone, indistinct articulation, indiscriminate slurring, non-observance of tempo, inaccurate note-values, poor grasp of harmony, and performance without feeling or sentiment.

Ex. 5.2. J. Haydn, Trumpet Concerto in E flat major Hob. VIIe/1, 1796: first movement, Allegro, trumpet (in B flat), bb. 37–44, suggested interpretation.

The importance of shaping and detaching longer note-values is illustrated in Ex. 5.2, from the opening solo of Haydn's Trumpet Concerto. The minims can easily sound too smooth, shapeless and out of character with the other musical ideas. The groups of slurred quavers should be detached from the notes that follow.

Ex. 5.3, from the first movement of Mozart's G major Flute Concerto K. 313, illustrates both long and short appoggiaturas – the latter normally dissonant, and requiring special emphasis and slight lengthening. Dissonance between the solo line and the underlying harmony forms an important aspect of the musical expression throughout this example, notably at the fourth bar. The small-scale phrasing is again important, and the long notes demand shape and character to match the surrounding music. A speech-like character is also important in slower movements, even where a more singing approach is appropriate.

Whether or not marked with a small grace note, trills in the music of Haydn and Mozart should normally begin on the upper note and should accelerate in truly ornamental fashion where this suits the character of the movement (Ex. 5.4). After about 1800, treatises began to recommend a trill beginning on the main note in certain circumstances, so for early nineteenth-century music either can be suitable, depending on the context.

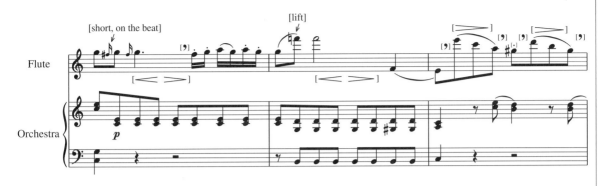

Ex. 5.3.
W. A. Mozart, Flute
Concerto in G major
K. 313, 1778: first
movement, Allegro
maestoso, bb. 164–9,
suggested interpreta-
tion.

Improvisation and cadenzas

Improvisation was an important part of performance in the Classical
period, when composer and performer, if not one and the same, were still
partners. Cadenzas were normally improvised: Quantz said that a wind
cadenza should be playable within one breath, but Tromlitz allowed some
exceptions to this rule. Melodies were most commonly decorated in slow
movements, although many writers advised players not to be too daring;
above all, a good knowledge of harmony was essential. Mozart's own ornamentation in his piano concertos provides models for similar treatment of
melodies in his wind concertos. Simple dance movements, such as the
minuets which form the finales of Mozart's Flute Concerto in G major and
his Bassoon Concerto, should also be decorated in repeated sections.

The value and necessity of tasteful ornamentation was certainly recognized, but we should remember ornamentation is a skill which could be
acquired only with much experience. By the beginning of the nineteenth
century it was gradually discouraged, as composers became more specific in their requirements. But when a composer and performer worked
closely together on solo music, their contributions could sometimes

Ex. 5.4.
W. A. Mozart, Sonata
in B flat major for
bassoon and cello
K. 292, c.1775:
second movement,
Andante, bb. 1–4,
suggested interpreta-
tion.

Fig. 5.7. Six-keyed
bassoons by Kusder,
London, *c*.1790 (left)
and Milhouse,
Newark, *c*.1780.

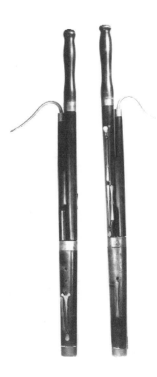

 become indistinguishable – for example in Weber's collaborations in his Clarinet concertos with the virtuoso Heinrich Baermann. All the same, it is important to avoid editions which include additions to the solo line by players of later generations.

Advice from the past

Classical wind treatises are full of all kinds of information and advice which even today seem immediately useful. Some writers made the important point that one should choose repertoire that is within one's capabilities, but admitted that no one could manage to play well at all times and in all circumstances. Quantz reckoned that it was important to know the mood of your audience, something not always possible in today's huge concert halls. Anton Stadler was more realistic, admitting that there was no accounting for the mood of an audience on a particular evening.

Some advice (like much historical evidence) needs to be interpreted with the conditions and tastes of the time in mind. An example is the treatise written by Joseph Fröhlich (*Vollständige theoretisch-praktische Musikschule*, 1810–11) for a new music school in Germany. Fröhlich's introduction now seems positively amusing, though it was intended quite seriously. He recommended for wind players a moderate lifestyle, and the avoidance of anything which could damage the chest, such as running, horseback riding, or the excessive consumption of hot drinks. He wrote that one should not practise after a meal, so the afternoon was best avoided; furthermore, one should not drink immediately after practising if the lungs were still warm, since this was the cause of many early deaths. In the case of dry lips – very bad for the embouchure – the mouth should be rinsed to give the lips new strength. It need hardly be said that Fröhlich was writing at a time when a performer's health was an altogether more fragile matter than it is today!

Richard Wigmore

Singing

Singers in the Classical period

An all too familiar complaint in this age of hype and exploitation is that singers are pressurized into doing too much too soon. Many of us can think of singers who have shot to stardom in their early twenties, and then, pushed by agents, opera managers and record company executives, and perhaps believing their own publicity, have taken on roles one or two sizes too heavy for them. The likely upshot is at best a loss of freshness and purity in the tone, at worst the start of slow vocal burn-out.

Any twenty-five-year-old today who tackles, say, Leonore in Beethoven's *Fidelio* or Agathe in Weber's *Der Freischütz* – both famously demanding roles for a lyric-dramatic soprano – is seriously tempting fate. Yet if we turn back two centuries we find, astonishingly, that the Austrian soprano Anna Milder-Hauptmann was just nineteen when she created Leonore in the original version of *Fidelio* in 1805, and that Wilhelmine Schröder-Devrient, destined to be one of the most celebrated divas of her time, scored triumphs

Fig. 6.1. Wilhelmine Schröder-Devrient, aged eighteen.

as both Leonore and Agathe before she reached her eighteenth birthday. The legendary Maria Malibran made her debut as Rosina in *Il barbiere di Siviglia* (The Barber of Seville) in London in 1825, also aged seventeen. Nor were these isolated exceptions. To take just a few of the singers Mozart worked with: both the first Countess Almaviva in *Le nozze di Figaro* (The Marriage of Figaro), Luisa Laschi, and the first Don Giovanni, Luigi Bassi, were barely twenty-one; Anna Gottlieb, the Charlotte Church of her day, sang Barbarina in the premiere of *Figaro* two days after her twelfth birthday, and was a seasoned professional by the time she appeared as Pamina in *Die Zauberflöte* (The Magic Flute) five years later; and in that opera even the part of Sarastro, with its associations of dignity and wisdom, was first taken by the twenty-six-year-old Franz Gerl, who four years earlier had scored a success in the formidable role of Osmin in *Die Entführung aus dem Serail* (The Abduction from the Seraglio).

That these singers were fully-fledged professionals at an age when their modern counterparts are still at school or music college certainly says something about their rigorous early training. Singers of 200 years ago, especially sopranos and tenors, did have an advantage in that pitch was around a semitone lower than it is today – and any aspiring Leonore will tell you what that means. But perhaps the crucial difference between an opera singer at the turn of the nineteenth century and one at the turn of the twenty-first lay in the sheer volume he or she was required to produce. In 1800 most concert halls and theatres were appreciably smaller than those built in the nineteenth and twentieth centuries; even more importantly, the singers of Mozart's and Beethoven's day did not have to compete with the weight and volume of the modern orchestra. With gut strings, played with minimal vibrato, and valveless brass, orchestral textures were much lighter and more transparent. And a gifted singer with a well-focused, well-projected voice could ride the fullest accompaniment without any need to force the tone – so often a trap for young singers today.

While a full, healthy resonance was always appreciated, the Classical period did not put a premium on vocal power as such. Singers were repeatedly praised for their roundness and sweetness of tone, their agility in florid passages, their command of both the 'brilliant' and the 'pathetic' styles, and their perfect control of nuance and ornament. In his *Musical Reminiscences* (1824), Richard, Earl Mount-Edgcumbe described Gasparo Pacchierotti, the outstanding castrato of the later eighteenth century, as follows:

> Pacchierotti's voice was an extensive soprano, full and sweet in the highest degree; his powers of execution were great, but he had far too good taste and too good sense to make a display of them where it would have been misapplied, confining it to one bravura aria in each opera, conscious that the chief delight of singing, and his own supreme excellence, lay in touching expression, and exquisite pathos.

Brigida Banti, one of the star prima donnas of the 1780s and 90s, despite a famously dissolute life style (she was reported to drink at least a bottle of wine each day), was praised in characteristically high-flown terms in the London *Morning Chronicle* in 1795:

> More perfect, more impassioned, more divine singing, perhaps, was never heard. The delicacy of her execution and sweetness of her taste and the enchanting discrimination of her feeling were incomparable.

'Discrimination', 'delicacy', 'taste', 'feeling': these critical buzzwords tell us something of the priorities of singers and their audiences in the late eighteenth century. And for many, the supreme test was a singer's skill and 'taste' in the execution of ornaments, including a perfect 'shake', or trill. Dr Charles Burney's comments on Elizabeth Billington, the first great English prima donna, are typical of the time:

> The natural tone of her voice is so exquisitely sweet, her knowledge of music so considerable, her shake so true, her closes and embellishments so true that nothing but envy or apathy can hear her without delight.

By the time Burney heard Elizabeth Billington, in the 1790s, the female soprano had eclipsed the male castrato in the vocal hierarchy; and with few exceptions it was now the prima donna rather than the eunuch who received the greatest adulation and commanded the biggest fees. The castrato survived in *opera seria*, the old-fashioned type of serious opera in Italian, right through the Classical period: Mozart composed the role of Sextus in his last opera, *La clemenza di Tito*, for a soprano castrato; even Rossini admired the purity and brilliance of the castrato voice and wrote one role for the last star of the breed, Giovanni Battista Velluti. But the castrato's heyday had passed by the 1780s, partly because the practice of castration was increasingly condemned, even in Italy, and partly because *opera seria*, traditionally the prime showcase for the castrato, was giving ground to the more democratic genres of *opera buffa* (Italian comic opera) and *Singspiel* (German opera with spoken dialogue).

Our own subdivisions within the basic voice-types did not exist in the late eighteenth century, which made no distinction between, say, a lyric and a *soubrette* soprano, or even between a soprano and a mezzo-soprano. In fact, the term mezzo-soprano did not exist: Dorabella in *Così fan tutte*, now almost invariably taken by a mezzo, was described as a soprano by Mozart and first sung by Louise Villeneuve, whose repertoire included coloratura (high and brilliant) soprano roles. Singers of Mozart's day had to be versatile: Luisa Laschi sang both Countess Almaviva and Zerlina in *Don Giovanni*, while the first Fiordiligi in *Così*, Adriana Ferrarese, had previously sung Susanna in *Figaro*, nowadays the province of the *soubrette*. Nor was there any formal distinction between bass and baritone. In *Don Giovanni*, for example, Leporello, Masetto, the Commendatore and the Don himself are all described as bass; and it is revealing that in the opera's premiere the contrasting roles of the Commendatore and Masetto were played by the same singer. A few German basses, such as Mozart's first Osmin, Ludwig Fischer, were specially admired for their cavernous low notes; and at the other end of the spectrum, some basses negotiated higher-lying roles by cultivating a head-voice upper extension, as tenors habitually did above an e' or f'. But it was only when Rossini began to write such roles as Figaro in *Il barbiere di Siviglia*, which consistently keeps the voice above the bass stave, that the baritone emerged as a separate vocal category between tenor and bass.

The triumph of the prima donna over the castrato in the late eighteenth century coincided with a new cult of spectacular high notes. From Lucrezia Agujari, unflatteringly known as 'La Bastardina', who in 1770 astonished the teenage Mozart with her C *in altissimo* (*c''''*, an octave above normal top C!), sopranos regularly dazzled audiences with their high-wire acts. Mozart takes both his sopranos in *Die Entführung* up to *e'''*, and the Queen of the Night up to *f'''*; and in a *scena* (concert scene) he wrote for his beloved Aloysia Weber, *Popoli di Tessaglia* K. 316, he goes one better by throwing in a *g'''*. Contemporary evidence suggests that most sopranos achieved these stratospheric heights by using a falsetto extension, probably similar to that heard on recordings made by Emma Calvé in the early years of the twentieth century.

Although we know that some tenors in the late eighteenth century sang up to *d''* and even *e''* in falsetto, composers rarely wrote for tenor higher than *a'* or *b♭'*. But in a number of Rossini roles the tenor not only achieved equal billing with the soprano – something virtually unheard-of in the previous century – but matched her in range and brilliance. Giovanni Davide, for instance, who sang in six Rossini premieres, was famed for his agility and three-octave compass, including a powerful head register. The roles Rossini composed for Davide contrast with the lower-lying tenor parts he wrote for Manuel García (the first Count Almaviva in *Il barbiere di Siviglia*) and Andrea Nozzari (the first Otello), both of whom traded on a strong, baritonal middle register.

Along with a growing differentiation between types of soprano – lyric, lyric-dramatic and coloratura – and types of tenor, and the appearance of the high baritone as a distinct category, the early nineteenth century also saw the emancipation of the female contralto voice. This had nothing in common with the sober, full-toned English oratorio contralto, but was rather the successor to the rapidly vanishing castrato: a brilliant, flexible, penetrating voice specializing in heroic male roles, such as Rossini's

Fig. 6.2. Interior of the King's Theatre, Haymarket, 1809, by J. Bluck after Rowlandson and Pagin.

Tancredi, as well as female parts like Rosina in *Il barbiere di Siviglia*. From the latter part of the nineteenth century few singers mustered the combination of richness, fire-eating virtuosity and sheer vocal range (from *g* up to *b″* or even *c‴*) required by the Rossini contralto; the true art of coloratura mezzo or contralto singing was revived, in spectacular style, only when Marilyn Horne came on the scene in the early 1960s.

Vocal technique

Probably the most influential treatise on singing written in the later eighteenth century was Giovanni Battista Mancini's *Pensieri, e riflessioni pratiche sopra il canto figurato* (Practical thoughts and reflections on singing), published in Vienna in 1774. Drawing on a famous earlier treatise by Pier Francesco Tosi (1723), Mancini, himself a castrato, laid down a number of precepts for perfect vocalism, which in the eighteenth century meant Italian vocalism. And much of what he wrote is as valid now as it was then. The prerequisites for any singer are a free and even production of tone, perfect intonation, flawless legato and immaculate control over the full dynamic range. Any constriction of the larynx, resulting in forced, guttural or nasal sounds, is anathema. The tone should flow easily on the breath, with the vibration of the vocal cords corresponding to the vibration of the strings on a violin or cello. Allied to the notion of singing on the breath is that of the correct place of resonance: a sound not sustained by the breath cannot take proper advantage of the resonating capacities of the head and the resonance chamber of the thorax. The voice of a performer singing on the breath gives the impression of being formed 'in the mask' (i.e. in the face); and the tone passes from *piano* to *forte*, and all dynamics in between, with such ease and spontaneity that the listener has the sensation that the tone is 'floating' on the breath.

Mancini also deals with the complex question of the *passaggio*, the change from chest to head, or falsetto, register. The aim was a seamless fusion of the two registers, with some of the characteristics of the chest voice blended into the falsetto register in the notes just above the *passaggio* in order to conceal the join. Right up to the age of Rossini tenors, baritones and basses generally sang above the *passaggio* – which occurs above middle C, somewhere between *d′* and *f′* – in head voice. But after the French tenor Gilbert Duprez (1806–96) began to carry the chest register up to top *c″* (to Rossini's horror, incidentally), high notes sung in chest voice – or, more accurately, a 'mixed voice' with a predominance of chest register – increasingly became the norm as singers began to compete with heavier orchestration. It is now unthinkable that a baritone singing Rossini's Figaro would take the high *e′*, *f′* and *g′* in head voice rather than in ringing chest tones.

Portamento and messa di voce

Two accomplishments expected of any half-decent singer in the Classical period were mastery of *messa di voce* – the capacity to swell the voice gradually from *piano* to *forte* and back again on sustained notes – and of *portamento di voce*, the smooth joining of notes by gliding imperceptibly over the intervening intervals. Nowadays we tend to view portamento in eighteenth- and early nineteenth-century music as something vulgar and anachronistic. But all the evidence is that it was as essential a part of the singer's armoury as it was of the string player's. A collection of annotated Mozart arias from about 1799, now in The British Library, suggests how a singer of the time may have applied portamento in slow and moderately paced numbers. As an example, below (Ex. 6.1) is the opening of one of Cherubino's arias from *Figaro*. The annotator indicates the use of portamento by adding short notes that anticipate the pitch of the following note. The notation suggests that the portamentos in the first bar were to be negotiated swiftly and lightly, to avoid any feeling of droopiness.

Ex. 6.1.
W. A. Mozart, *Le nozze di Figaro* (1786): Act II, scene ii, 'Voi, che sapete', bb. 9–10, with version from a manuscript of *c*.1799, showing use of portamento.

In his *The Singer's Preceptor* (1810), the composer and singing master Domenico Corri uses short anticipatory notes in small type to indicate portamento. These notes were not intended to convey any precise rhythmic definition.

Ex. 6.2. D. Corri, *The Singer's Preceptor* (1810): J. Haydn, 'She never told her love', 1794, bb. 15–17.

Portamento continued to be used by singers throughout the nineteenth century and into the twentieth; we can hear it effectively applied in early twentieth-century recordings of Emma Eames singing 'Gretchen am Spinnrade', or the French bass Pol Plançon in 'In diesen heil'gen Hallen' from *Die Zauberflöte* – both of which may well be closer to what Schubert and Mozart expected than the portamento-free style of most singers today. While it is hard for us to apply portamento as naturally as did the singers of 100 and 200 years ago, it is certainly worth practising it, with restraint, on particularly expressive intervals in slower arias, especially those of a soulful or tragic character like the Countess's 'Porgi amor' or Pamina's 'Ach, ich fühl's'.

Messa di voce (literally 'placing of the voice'), revealing a perfect control of the slow crescendo and diminuendo, was an equally crucial aspect of the singer's art. According to Mancini, it was invariably used on long held notes at the beginning of an aria, on any note with a fermata that was left undecorated, and at the beginning of a cadenza. He adds: 'A truly accomplished singer will use it on every long note that occurs in a cantilena'. Exactly what constitutes a 'long note' is debatable; and in any case, even if you have perfectly mastered *messa di voce*, you should beware of overusing the device and creating too many bulges in the line. But there is no question that the examples in Ex. 6.3, from a soprano aria in Haydn's *Creation*, cry out for the use of *messa di voce*.

Vibrato

The question of vocal vibrato in the Classical period is a tricky one for us today. All the evidence indicates that until at least the mid-nineteenth

century, singers usually sang with minimal natural vibrato. Conscious oscillation on longer notes was occasionally used for special 'tremulant' effects; and in the early nineteenth century voluntary vibrato was sometimes applied in passages of extreme emotion. But for the most part, pronounced fluctuation of pitch and intensity on sustained notes was deplored. (See Chapter 2 'Notation and Interpretation', p. 33, for Mozart's comments on the Salzburg singer Josef Meissner and his 'bad habit of making his voice tremble at times'.)

Ex. 6.3. J. Haydn, *The Creation*, 1796–8: 'On mighty pens' (a) bb. 63–9; (b) bb. 152½–7.

The problem for us is that until the 'early music' revolution and the appearance of ultra-light, 'specialist' sopranos of the Emma Kirkby school, the general tendency during the twentieth century was for singers, like string players, to cultivate a wider, more intense vibrato. With little doubt, most modern singers of Mozart, Rossini or Schubert have a stronger natural vibrato than their counterparts of two centuries ago: the voice may 'tremble at times', but it trembles more intensely than in Mozart's day. Purity and steadiness of tone, with no hint of wobble, are certainly highly desirable in all music of the Classical period. But few singers can suppress their natural vibrato without impairing freedom of production; and in any case, a degree of vibrato is virtually essential today if you want to be heard against a modern orchestra in a large hall or theatre.

Interpreting the text

The notion that a composer's written text is sacrosanct is very much a twentieth-century phenomenon. Until recently ignorance of Classical conventions and the cult of absolute fidelity to the printed score meant that interpreters failed to provide ornamentation and even basic appoggiaturas that would have been second nature to performers of Mozart's and Rossini's day. Even in our own authenticity-conscious age, when so much more is known about Classical performance practice, singers often fight shy of obligatory embellishments and observe appoggiaturas at best haphazardly.

Appoggiaturas

In the Classical, as in the Baroque, period, basic appoggiaturas – literally 'leaning notes' – were added to the composer's written text as a matter of course: there was no question of the appoggiatura being an optional ornament. In both recitative and aria a performer would have automatically applied an appoggiatura when so-called feminine endings – i.e. a pair of notes, the first accented, the second weak, followed by a pause – are written as two notes at the same pitch. The most usual instances are: 1) when the

Ex. 6.4.
W. A. Mozart, *Così fan tutte* (1790): Act I, scene iii, recitative, bb. 3–8.

voice falls by a 3rd or a 2nd to the final note, as at (a) and (c) of Ex. 6.4 – here the appoggiatura is sung on the note above the tonic, as indicated above Mozart's notation; and 2) when it falls by a 4th to the dominant, the characteristic ending for a recitative. Here the tonic is repeated, as at the end of Ex. 6.5. Appoggiaturas from below, while less common, are also advocated by Classical theorists, especially when the words convey a question, as at (b) and (d) in Ex. 6.4.

Ex. 6.5. J. Haydn, *The Creation*: recitative 'And God created man', original German text, from b. 6.

A literal reproduction of what the composer wrote in the above examples would have seemed ugly and ungrammatical to Haydn's and Mozart's contemporaries; and there is no excuse for anyone to omit the appoggiaturas today. More debatable is the insertion of appoggiaturas on masculine endings (i.e. a single, accented note), as at (e) in Ex. 6.4. Theorists give many examples of these, while warning against the dangers of monotony if they are overused: as in so many things at the time, singers were expected to be guided by their taste and discretion.

The use of appoggiaturas in arias and even in ensemble music was – and is – no less obligatory, as you can see in this extract (Ex. 6.6) from Fiordiligi's 'Come scoglio' in *Così fan tutte*.

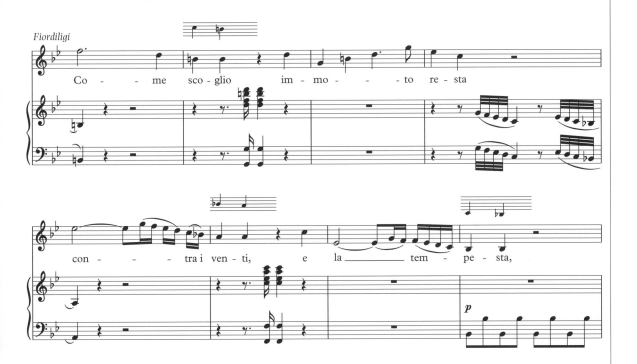

This aria, like many others, has numerous 'blunt endings' that absolutely demand appoggiaturas. But until recent performances and recordings directed by the likes of Charles Mackerras, Arnold Östman and John Eliot Gardiner, the notes were habitually sung exactly as Mozart wrote them.

Ex. 6.6.
W. A. Mozart, *Così fan tutte*: Act I, scene xi, 'Come scoglio', bb. 58–65.

Embellishing arias

The Baroque practice of decorating the da capo, or repeated first section, of an aria carried over into the Classical period, even though by this time strict da capo (ABA) form was being superseded by more flexible patterns. While theorists disagreed, sometimes vehemently, about how elaborately a line should be decorated, it was second nature for singers to add some degree of embellishment when a section was recapitulated, or even just a part of the vocal line repeated: judging from surviving contemporary examples of ornamentation, it seems to have been an unwritten rule that repeats were never identical. To take an instance from one of the most famous arias of the period, Ex. 6.7 is the final return of the melody of 'Che farò' from Gluck's *Orfeo ed Euridice* as ornamented by Domenico Corri.

Ex. 6.7. D. Corri, extract from *A Select Collection of the Most Admired Songs, Duetts etc.* (*c.*1779). In keeping with what Corri advocates elsewhere, the embellishments here are quite restrained, mainly added appoggiaturas for 'pathetic' effect, plus paired grace notes (a) and turns, or *gruppetti* (b); note, too, Corri's suggested breathing marks, breaking the line into smaller units than you would normally expect in a performance today.

Gluck, we know, had a crusade to rid opera of what he regarded as irrelevant excrescences, including extravagant, crowd-pleasing ornamentation. But though we do not know exactly how much embellishment Gluck himself sanctioned, the fairly modest ornamentation in the example above – as opposed to the wholesale rewriting of the melodic lines sometimes heard today – would have been regarded as 'tasteful execution' by eighteenth-century listeners. It is certainly a useful guide for us, though as with portamento, a safe rule is: if in doubt, do less rather than more.

Embellishments were not confined to repeated lines or sections in the Classical period. Various contemporary sources indicate that slow, cantabile arias were often decorated from the outset. In Ex. 6.8 the original melodic line from a concert aria by Mozart is placed below the embellished version he made for Aloysia Weber. Notice how Mozart adds appoggiaturas – some, though not all, demanded by musical grammar – at the beginning of most bars and, as in the Gluck example above, never permits identical repeated phrases. Mozart's embellishments here, quite discreet by the standards of some surviving eighteenth-century examples, are an obvious model for any singer today in a cantabile aria of the period.

In fast arias decoration was, understandably, applied more sparingly. Appoggiaturas were often added; and other devices found in contemporary sources – which I would recommend only to singers with the most confident command of period style – included syncopations to enliven the rhythm, and the filling out of longer notes with semiquaver running passages. Two generally observed conventions in Mozart's day were that wide leaps in long notes were left undecorated (Fiordiligi's 'Come scoglio', again, has several such instances), and that – unlike in some modern performances – singers did not transpose their lines up an octave to show off their high notes.

Though there were no hard and fast divisions, it is safe to say that operatic arias were subject to more ornamentation than sacred music or songs, and that Italian opera was more freely embellished – with correspondingly greater freedom of rhythm – than German. We know that Haydn, in *The Creation*, preferred a minimum of decoration, confined mainly to fermatas and cadenzas (see below). And the generally simpler style of the arias in *Die Zauberflöte* make them less suitable for ornamentation than those of, say, *Figaro* or *Così*. In fact an anecdote by Joseph Carl Schikaneder, nephew of the librettist and original Papageno, relates how Mozart bridled when Franz Gerl tried to embellish Sarastro's 'In diesen heil'gen Hallen' in a rehearsal:

'Stop, Gerl. If I'd wanted to have it like that, I'd have written it that way'.

Rossini often wrote his ornamentation into the score for a particular singer, as did Mozart in the concert aria quoted above. The most popular aria form by this time was the combination of cavatina and cabaletta, with florid embellishments both in the (slow) cavatina section and in the repeats of the closing (fast) cabaletta. Rossini and other composers make increasing play with added high notes, especially in the coda of the cabaletta where the singer's virtuosity is given free rein. Ex. 6.9 (overleaf) shows the end of Rosina's 'Una voce poco fà' as first written and as Rossini later elaborated it: a reminder that only mezzos with a first-class coloratura technique should begin to contemplate this and other similar Rossini roles.

Ex. 6.8.
W. A. Mozart, 'Non sò d'onde viene' K. 294, 1778: bb. 14–28.

Fermatas and cadenzas

In the Classical and early Romantic periods decoration at fermatas – pauses where the accompaniment is temporarily silent – was as obligatory as the addition of appoggiaturas on blunt endings. The minimum expected embellishment was a display of *messa di voce*, as in Ex. 6.3; more often, singers improvised a short flourish or miniature cadenza. The most emphatic fermatas are commonly found just before the return to the main theme of an aria. To give you an idea of what was expected, Ex. 6.10 is from a

Ex. 6.9. G. Rossini,
Il barbiere di Siviglia
(1816): Act I, scene ix,
'Una voce poco fà',
bb. 107–14.

famous aria in Mozart's *Il re pastore*, in which the composer wrote out his own embellishment at the lead-back to the main theme.

Ex. 6.10.
W. A. Mozart,
Il re pastore (1775):
Act II, scene vi,
'L'amerò', bb. 85–7.

Surviving parts for early performances of *The Creation* give us a unique insight into what Haydn himself sanctioned in the way of ornamentation: all the added embellishments are modest, those for the tenor and bass soloists even more so than those for the soprano. The two examples of fermatas in Ex. 6.11 show the bare minimum of decoration added.

Ex. 6.11. J. Haydn,
The Creation: 'With
verdure clad'
(a) bb. 29–33;
(b) bb. 84–8.

Elaborate vocal cadenzas at fermatas were normally reserved for the close of both the A and the B sections of da capo arias, found primarily in *opera seria*. The character of a cadenza was expected to match that of the aria; and a rule observed in theory, if not invariably in practice, was that the cadenza should be taken in one breath – though we should bear in mind that many singers of the period were famed for phenomenal feats of breath control. Cadenzas enabled singers to display their florid technique, their perfect trill and, often, their mastery of chromatic intervals and wide leaps. The following 'model' cadenza, Ex. 6.12, is cited by Mancini – though even in those days no soprano, surely, would have encompassed it in a single breath.

Ex. 6.12. From G. B. Mancini, *Pensieri, e riflessioni pratiche sopra il canto figurato* (1774).

Thankfully, not all surviving cadenzas of the period are as fearsome as this!

Recitative

From the writings of theorists in the Classical period we know that recitative was treated quite freely, and inflected according to the stresses of speech. Mancini provided a useful pointer to the interpretation of recitative when he wrote that the notated rhythm should be 'loosened so that it resembles a perfect and simple spoken declamation'. The speed was determined by the dramatic situation, and was naturally faster in *opera buffa* than in *opera seria* or oratorio. But although the rhythm might be 'loosened', rests were apparently always observed in the more formal, declamatory recitative of *opera seria* – a practice not followed in many modern performances and recordings of, say, Mozart's *Idomeneo* or *La clemenza di Tito*. The addition of appoggiaturas was, of course, compulsory; and fermatas were often a cue for a brief embellishment, such as we find in the authentic performing parts for *The Creation*. Below is the close of the recitative for Adam and Eve in Part 3.

Ex. 6.13. J. Haydn, *The Creation*: recitative 'Our duty we have now performed', bb. 36–8.

Lieder

We have little precise information about the performance of lieder (songs with piano) during this period – for obvious reasons. Until the second half of the nineteenth century lieder singing was essentially an amateur, domestic art that took place in small, private salons. Few professional opera singers gave public performances of lieder; and the only one to do so regularly in the 1820s, Johann Michael Vogl, had virtually retired from the stage when he began to champion Schubert's songs. We can be pretty sure that most performances were direct and unsophisticated, with the emphasis on clear enunciation of the text: the subtle coloration and psychological probing of a Dietrich Fischer-Dieskau or a Brigitte Fassbaender is very much a late twentieth-century phenomenon. When Schubert sang through his own songs in his light, falsetto-ish tenor, he always kept strictly in time; and we know from the memoirs of a close friend, Leopold von Sonnleithner, that 'he never tolerated violent expression in lieder singing'. We also know that Vogl applied the same kind of interpretative freedom to lieder singing that he would have used in opera, adding ornaments, varying repeats and even inserting rests or altering the melodic line for dramatic effect. Some of Schubert's friends objected to Vogl's more extravagant excesses; but there is evidence that Schubert approved of his 'small alterations and embellishments'. Discreet ornamentation of lieder, confined mainly to added trills and turns, can certainly be effective, though few modern singers attempt it: two exceptions are the tenor Ernst Haefliger and the baritone Max van Egmond in their recordings of *Winterreise*, both accompanied on a piano of Schubert's day.

Fig. 6.3. 'Schubertiad' at Josef von Spaun's. Vogl is singing and Schubert playing the piano. Artist and date unknown.

Ensemble and choral singing

As with lieder, little was written about ensemble and choral singing in the Classical and early Romantic periods. The freedom of interpretation applied to solo music was obviously out of the question when two or more voices were involved, although solo singers in ensembles would add a modest number of trills and appoggiaturas. If a composer wanted a cadenza in a duet, as in 'Ah perdona' from *La clemenza di Tito*, he would write it out. Except for basic appoggiaturas, embellishments were even less expected of choral singers.

Female sopranos were banned from singing in church choirs in both Catholic and Protestant countries, although they sometimes sang the solo parts in church performances, as in Mozart's C minor Mass in Salzburg in 1783, or in Haydn's late masses the following decade – a practice frowned on by some puritanical commentators. In England the tradition of oratorio performances using huge, mixed-voiced choirs (with women and perhaps some boy sopranos, and countertenors on the alto line) began with the Handel celebrations of 1784. But in Austria oratorio choirs remained all-male, with boy sopranos and boy altos, until the founding of the mixed-voiced Gesellschaft der Musikfreunde in Vienna in 1814.

The first Viennese public performances of *The Creation* around the turn of the nineteenth century numbered around 200 participants, with an orchestra of about 130 and an (all-male) choir of about 70 – a ratio which reverses that of the average choral society performance today, though we should remember that the instruments of the time were less sonorous than their modern equivalents. In England and France, choirs and orchestras tended to be about equal in size; and there are reports of gargantuan performances, especially in Paris, with 300 or more singers and players. Many performances, of course, were far more modest. But the common assumption that authentic automatically equals small-scale in the Classical era is far from the whole truth.

Barry Cooper

Sources and Editions

Introduction

Many performers, when confronted with the printed score of a piece of music by Haydn, Beethoven, or one of their contemporaries, assume rather naively that the music in front of them coincides exactly with what the composer originally wrote and intended. Regrettably, this is not always the case even with recent works, and it is rarely true of music written some 200 years ago. Even major works which have been subject to intensive study by scholars often appear in unsatisfactory editions. An awareness of how an edition has been prepared, however, and of the problems that faced the editor, can result in the performer gaining a much greater understanding of the music being performed. This in turn can lead to more effective performances.

Modern editions of music from the so-called Classical period can be divided into three types: 'performing' editions, 'scholarly' editions, and what might be called 'scholarly performing' editions. Pure performing editions generally contain helpful hints on how the editor thinks the music should be interpreted. The editor, who may be a well-known performer, will indicate such matters as bowing, breathing, fingering, phrasing, pedalling or recommended dynamic levels, often disregarding what the composer actually wrote. Thus the version presented will reflect the editor's preferences rather than the composer's. In scholarly editions, on the other hand, care is taken to present as faithfully as possible exactly what the composer wrote. These editions present a generally reliable musical text, but without indicating how that music was actually intended to sound. Such editions are often described as 'Urtext' (literally 'original text'), to distinguish them from performing editions; but the word 'Urtext' has in some cases been debased through editorial additions, and the validity of the whole concept of an Urtext has been questioned, since 'what the composer wrote' is not always certain.

Some editions, however, combine the best features of both of the previous two types. After establishing the composer's own version as far as possible, the editor explains in a preface, and perhaps on the actual music pages, what sounds the notation was intended to convey. Contrary to popular assumption, notation has changed considerably since the eighteenth century, and in addition there were a great many unwritten conventions, concerning such matters as instruments, articulation and dynamics, that need to be learnt by performers familiar only with the conventions of today. Thus a good edition should contain both a reliable musical text as intended by the composer, and a reliable guide to how to interpret and perform that text. The question of interpreting the text is discussed in earlier chapters (especially Chapter 2 'Notation and Interpretation'). The problem of obtaining a reliable text is a central issue of the present chapter.

Sources

All editions of Classical music are based on one or more sources that provide the editor with the basic material. To understand what types of sources there are, it is best to think of how a work was transmitted from the composer's mind to our modern edition. The work originated as a group or succession of ideas, which the composer might try out first on his instrument. Beethoven is known to have composed extensively at the piano on occasion, before writing down a single note. Such activity, of course, leaves no written record and so provides no source for the modern editor. The composer might then have made some rough drafts or sketches for the work. Beethoven often sketched very extensively, and many of his sketches still survive, whereas Mozart and Haydn sketched far less and seem often to have discarded any sketches they did make. Since all sketches represent preliminary work rather than the final product, they are rarely of any use to an editor attempting to establish the text of a work. Occasionally, however, they can help to confirm minor details in a final score: for example, if an editor suspects that there is a sharp missing in the score, then the presence of that sharp in a sketch will tend to confirm these suspicions.

After completing any sketches, the composer eventually wrote down the whole work for the first time, using pre-ruled manuscript paper. This score is known as the 'autograph score', whether or not the composer actually signed his name on it. Occasionally the term 'holograph' is also used, and in this context effectively denotes the same thing. The autograph score, being the first place where the work was written down complete, is of fundamental importance, since all other sources are based on it directly or indirectly. But, as we shall see, it is by no means the only source that needs to be considered. In any case, the autograph score may not necessarily survive. In general, the earlier the music, the more likely it is that the autograph has disappeared. For most of Haydn's early works there is no known autograph. The same applies to many of Beethoven's early works, although his later works are well represented. For Schubert, however, the autograph is often the only source, since many of his works remained unpublished and virtually unknown until long after his death.

Sometimes a composer made changes while writing out the autograph. This was less common for Mozart and Haydn than for Beethoven, whose manuscripts occasionally became so messy that a whole movement or work was written out a second time. In his Piano Sonata Op. 110, for example, the finale exists in two autograph scores, which can conveniently be referred to as the 'composing score' and 'fair copy'. On other occasions, a composer decided to revise a work some time after it had been completed and perhaps published, in which case there may have been a composing score and/or fair copy for each version. Where more than one version of a work survives it is customary to regard the final version as the official one, representing the composer's latest thoughts and superseding earlier ones, unless it is demonstrably some makeshift version adapted to the needs of a particular performance.

Sometimes, after completing the autograph, the composer arranged for a professional copyist to make a fair copy – usually either a set of parts for a performance, or a score to be sent to a publisher for printing. The best copyists reached a very high standard of accuracy, but they were bound to make occasional errors, perhaps where the autograph was insufficiently clear. Many of Beethoven's works were copied in this way, and Beethoven himself would then correct the copy. His corrections covered not only errors made by the copyist but also the addition of slurs, accidentals, etc., that had mistakenly been omitted in the original autograph. He also sometimes made minor revisions at this stage. Thus these corrected copies often provide a better text than the autograph; but they might also include copying errors missed during checking.

Before the eighteenth century most music was circulated through manuscript copies rather than printed editions, but during the course of that century improvements in technology made music printing gradually easier and cheaper, so that printed music became increasingly common. Thus modern editors of music from the Classical period often have to contend with a mixture of printed and manuscript sources. Music printing was normally done through engraved metal plates, but other methods, notably lithography, were introduced during this period. The shift towards printing is striking. Bach wrote over 200 cantatas but only one was printed during his lifetime; and his *Das wohltemperirte Clavier* (The Well-Tempered Clavier) was not printed until long after his death, even though many manuscript copies were in circulation. In contrast, nearly all of Beethoven's sonatas were published within two years of being composed. Mozart and Haydn occupied an intermediate place in this respect: their early works were normally disseminated through manuscript copies, at least initially, but many of their later works were printed during their lifetimes. Meanwhile, Clementi actually founded a publishing firm and could therefore print his own compositions at any time. Schubert, however, being relatively young and unknown even at the time of his death, often had difficulty persuading publishers to print his works, and so many of them remained in manuscript. Whether a work was published also depended partly on its genre: operas and church music were less likely to be published than sonatas or variations.

If a composer wanted a work to be printed, he sent either the autograph score or a corrected copy to the publisher, and a set of plates was engraved from this. A single trial copy, known as a 'proof', was produced, and either checked by the publisher or sent to the composer for checking. The plates were then amended, before further copies were produced. If the checking was done by the composer, it was still possible for him to make an improvement even at this late stage. A famous example of this occurs in Beethoven's 'Waldstein' Sonata Op. 53: the autograph, which contains marks indicating it was used as the engraver's copy, shows an $f\flat$ for the left hand at the start of bar 105 (Ex. 7.1), but the flat is missing in the original (i.e. first) edition. A modern editor might assume this was a careless oversight, but close inspection of the original edition shows an amendment to the plate at this point, with the flat carefully deleted – evidently on Beethoven's instructions.

Ex. 7.1. Beethoven, 'Waldstein' Sonata Op. 53, 1803–4, autograph score: first movement, Allegro con brio, bb. 104–5.

Once the proof copy and the plates had been amended, a run of usually 50 or 100 copies was produced. The plates were then stored, and further runs were produced at later dates if required. Between runs, plates were occasionally amended again as mistakes came to light; and individual plates that were wearing out were replaced with new ones, thereby introducing the possibility of fresh errors. Thus editors cannot assume, as most have done, that all copies of a printed edition with the same title pages are identical. Ideally, every known copy of the original edition should be checked, though in practice this is not always feasible. Conversely, two early editions with different title pages, perhaps even from different publishers, sometimes prove to have been printed from a single set of plates (plates were sometimes transferred from one publisher to another).

If a work proved successful it was sometimes copied by a rival publisher, or by one in another country. Copyright laws within individual countries were still fairly rudimentary, and there was no international copyright law. Thus most of these later editions were quite legal, even though the composer derived no direct benefit from them. They are little use as sources, however, since they contain all but the most obvious errors of the original edition and generally introduce several new ones. Occasionally, however, a composer supervised two editions from different publishers – generally from different countries. Both Haydn and Beethoven managed to sell some of their works to both an English and an Austrian publisher, thereby gaining two fees. In the case of Beethoven's piano sonatas Op. 31, the composer received no proofs from the original publisher, Nägeli of Zurich, and found the first edition full of mistakes. He immediately asked his pupil Ferdinand Ries to make a list of mistakes and send it to another publisher, Simrock of Bonn, who printed a corrected version. Clementi's sonatas Op. 40 even have three authentic editions. The work was first published in London by Clementi's own firm, but he took the score to Paris and authorized a new edition by Pleyel, which contains a few significant variants; he then took the score to Vienna, where he authorized a third edition, by Mollo, again with slight changes.

If a composer did not have a work published shortly after its composition, people usually began making manuscript copies. Sometimes such a copy was authorized by the composer, and made by someone who had close connections with him, in which case its text is generally fairly accurate. But where second-hand and third-hand copies were made, as with many of Haydn's early works, the text being transmitted became increasingly unreliable; yet these may be the only sources that survive. Sometimes a publisher used such unreliable sources as the basis for an edition, though this was increasingly rare towards the end of the Classical period, when publishers more often dealt directly with composers. Often it is unclear how much supervision, if any, a composer exercised over particular printed editions, but if they date from the composer's lifetime there is generally at least a theoretical possibility that they had some connection with him. Sources dating from after the composer's death, however, generally have less value, since the composer could not have had any direct input.

In rare cases there may be other types of source, such as lists of corrections sent by the composer to the publisher; but the main possibilities can be summarized as follows:

1 sketches and rough drafts;
2 composing score ⎫
3 composer's fair copy ⎭ autograph scores;
4 corrected copy, prepared by copyist with composer's annotations;
5 edition (possibly more than one) supervised by composer;
6 manuscript copy closely associated with composer;
7 other manuscript copies from composer's lifetime;
8 other printed editions from composer's lifetime;
9 posthumous manuscripts or printed editions.

Assessment of sources

It is almost unknown for all nine types of source to survive for a single work. For many works, one or more sources may be lost; for others, certain categories may never have existed in the first place. In any good modern edition the editor should list all the sources known to have existed, including any now missing, and should have consulted all those available – either the originals themselves or at least photocopies or microfilms of them. Wherever a work from the Classical period survives in more than one source, there will almost certainly be differences in the text, known as 'variants'. From study of all the sources and especially their variants, the editor should have tried to work out the relationships between them, and produced a kind of family tree, known as a 'stemma' (plural 'stemmata'), showing these relationships. Literary editors working on texts of the Middle Ages or classical antiquity have been aware of this problem for many decades, and for them the study of stemmata has become quite a sophisticated science. Much music editing, however, has been done by musicians who, while excellent performers, have no training in scientific editorial methods; thus they may merely list the sources or refer vaguely to manuscripts and original editions. Indeed it is surprisingly rare to find a modern edition that contains a full assessment of the relationships between all the sources.

Sometimes the stemma will be quite straightforward; with other works it can be quite complex, especially if the composer has made significant revisions. Two examples follow. In the case of Mozart's Piano Sonata in C major K. 309 the autograph is lost, but there are four sources which are probably independent of each other. If they are, then the stemma is:

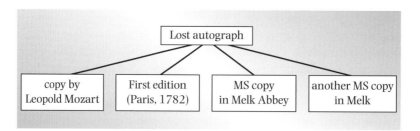

It is rarely possible to confirm that one source derives directly from a preceding one unless there is some external evidence; nearly always there could be an intervening source now lost. Thus, in the above example, the Melk copies and the Paris edition may well have been prepared from sources now lost, although ultimately they must derive from an autograph score. Hypothetical intervening sources may be omitted from stemmata.

For the first movement of Beethoven's last piano sonata, Op. 111, the picture is rather more complicated and not entirely certain. The autograph score was revised after having been copied by Wenzel Rampl; Rampl's copy was used for a Paris edition produced by Moritz Schlesinger, which Beethoven proof-read. Meanwhile Beethoven wrote out a fair copy of the revised version and sent this to London, where it was used for Clementi's edition. A third edition, produced in Vienna by Cappi & Diabelli, was evidently based on this same fair copy and Schlesinger's edition, which was later reissued with further corrections. Thus there are several differences or variants between the various sources, and none coincides exactly with Beethoven's final intentions, which may not even have been firmly established in all cases. A probable stemma (slightly simplified) is shown below – but remember that Beethoven was directly involved in all the sources except the Clementi edition.

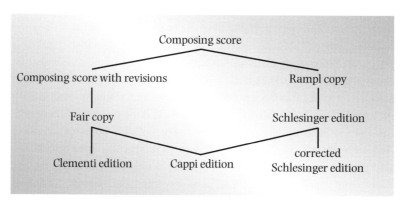

If a source can be shown to derive exclusively from another known source, as happens in the above case with the Clementi edition, then it loses its significance and can be discarded by the editor, since any differences from its model are due not to the composer but to some other cause. All other sources, however, are taken into account by the editor in the best modern editions.

Variants

Although variants are a great help in establishing the relationship between sources, they can be an enormous problem when the editor is trying to recreate the composer's intended text. The task of selecting the correct form of each passage where such variants occur requires a high degree of skill, knowledge and musical judgement. It is unsatisfactory to include a random mixture of variants from different sources; but relying on only one of several sources is almost as bad, unless all the other sources can be shown to derive exclusively from that source (as happens, for example, when an autograph score survives, along with several inaccurate copies of it). The editor should ideally work out the cause of each variant, and thereby base the text of the new edition on what he or she believes to be the composer's final intentions. In music of the Classical period there are a number of possible causes of variants, which can be categorized as follows:

1. corruption of the text, caused by simple miscopying;
2. degeneration of the text, caused by accidental omission of details such as slurs or ornaments;
3. distortion, through a copyist's deliberate alteration, perhaps simplifying or updating the music;
4. correction, or attempted correction, of obvious errors;
5. revisions made by the composer;
6. amplification of the text through additional performance indications such as metronome marks;
7. faulty memorization of a work, when it is being written out from memory (this sometimes happens when a composer writes out part of a recapitulation without checking that it corresponds exactly to the exposition);
8. notational changes intended to clarify the appearance of the music without affecting its sound.

There is a slight overlap between some of these categories, and it is not always possible to be sure which one is responsible for a particular variant. But a systematic application of these principles to each individual variant can greatly assist the editor's attempts to obtain the most reliable text. Often, however, it is impossible to prove which version was intended by the composer, and so the variants that are not incorporated into the editor's final music text should be listed in what is known variously as a critical commentary, textual commentary, critical report, or *Revisionsbericht*. Performers can then see for themselves how the text they are to perform was established, and in some cases they may reach a different opinion about what the composer intended. Critical commentaries are generally dense and filled with abbreviations, making daunting reading. Performers, however, are well advised to consult them, especially in places where the musical text presented seems slightly odd. Often they will help explain some irregularity.

Whether the edition is based on only one or on several sources, there may well be places where the sources contain an error. Some errors are more definite than others. In Beethoven's *Sonate pathétique*, for example, the left hand at bar 133 of the first movement is notationally incorrect in the original edition, containing insufficient note-values (Ex. 7.2). Obviously either a dot is missing after the rest or the final note should be a semi-quaver; comparison with parallel passages indicates that the dot is missing and should be added editorially (there is also a dot missing in the right hand in the same bar – can you see where?). Other errors have produced versions that are theoretically possible but clearly lie outside the style of the period – such as absurd discords. An example of this occurs near the start of Beethoven's 'Moonlight' Sonata (Ex. 7.3). This part of the autograph score, like that of the *Pathétique*, is lost, and the only source is the first edition: although bar 11 is playable as it stands, the absence of naturals before the two Ds in the left hand is clearly an oversight.

Ex. 7.2. Beethoven, *Sonate pathétique* Op. 13, first edition (1799): first movement, Grave – Allegro di molto e con brio, bb. 133–5.

Ex. 7.3. Beethoven, 'Moonlight' Sonata Op. 27 No. 2, first edition (1802): first movement, Adagio sostenuto, bb. 5½–15.

In other cases, however, the situation is more doubtful: there may be an odd harmony that is unlikely but not quite impossible, or an exposition and recapitulation that do not quite match in some tiny detail, for no obvious reason. In Beethoven's 'Hammerklavier' Sonata there is a famous passage (bars 224–6; see Ex. 7.4) where again some naturals have apparently been omitted in the first edition. Some editors have argued that Beethoven may have intended a highly bizarre effect, with A♯s, at this point. This argument, however, is unconvincing, especially in view of the obviously missing natural sign in bar 222 (left hand).

Most editors have also assumed that the right hand should be displaced to sound one quaver later in bars 224–6. Here the position is more tricky. Some editors silently 'correct' such passages, perhaps covering themselves by saying for example: 'Obvious errors have been corrected without comment'. This clause, however, can cover a great range of possibilities, and should immediately make the performer wary of the edition. Other editors simply leave all such errors uncorrected, claiming that the role of

Ex. 7.4. Beethoven, 'Hammerklavier' Sonata Op. 106, first edition (1819): first movement, Allegro, bb. 220–27.

the editor is simply to transmit what is in the sources. Performers should be equally wary of this attitude, which really just reflects a misplaced devotion to the incompetence of eighteenth-century copyists and engravers, nearly all of whom made frequent mistakes. A good editor, however, will correct everything that is believed to be erroneous, and indicate that this has been done. If the editorial amendment is the addition of something that had been omitted, such as a tie or an accidental, it can be indicated in the music text itself: the standard way is to use such means as dotted or crossed ties, small notes and accidentals, and square brackets (the use of these devices should be explained in the editorial introduction). If the amendment is more complicated, or is a general principle, it should be mentioned in the critical commentary or introduction, or by an explanatory note on the page itself. Thus it should always be possible for the performer to reconstruct what was in the original sources – or at least what was in the main source used – from the information supplied in the edition.

Choosing your edition

By now it should be clear what points to look out for when choosing which edition to use for performance. The main points can be covered in a series of questions:

1 Does the edition list all the sources, including the names of the libraries where they are held, so that the performer can consult them directly if necessary?
2 Has the editor understood and explained the relationships between all the sources?
3 Are the editorial methods and procedures clearly stated?
4 If they are stated, are they sound and rigorous – not placing too much reliance on one source, for example?
5 Is there a critical commentary?
6 Is any editorial material in the musical text clearly distinguished as such?
7 Could you retrieve the text in the original sources (or at least the best original source) from the information provided?
8 Is the musical text accurately and clearly printed, with satisfactory layout regarding such things as page turns?

9 Are there notes on performance practice, explaining any notational peculiarities such as ornament signs, and indications as to how the composer would have wanted the work to be performed, as far as is known?

There are remarkably few editions for which the answer is 'yes' to all nine questions, and performers may have to be satisfied with something less than ideal for the time being. Many major works have still not appeared in an edition that is ideal in every way, though conversely some works by relatively minor composers have appeared in editions that are wholly admirable. In general the most reliable editions are those that appear in major scholarly series such as *Musica Britannica* or *The London Pianoforte School*, or in collected editions of the main composers. For the four most celebrated composers of the Classical period the collected editions are:

Haydn: *Werke*, edited by the Joseph-Haydn-Institut, Cologne, published by Henle. This series is still far from complete. Haydn's keyboard sonatas are also available as *Klaviersonaten*, ed. Georg Feder, 3 vols (Munich, 1972), based on the collected edition, and as *Sämtliche Klaviersonaten*, ed. Christa Landon, 3 vols (Vienna: Universal, 1964–6), though the latter edition publishes the editorial report separately.

Mozart: *Neue Ausgabe sämtlicher Werke*, edited by the Internationale Stiftung Mozarteum, Salzburg, published by Bärenreiter. This edition supersedes the collected edition produced in the nineteenth century. For the piano sonatas, Stanley Sadie's edition (published by the Associated Board of the Royal Schools of Music) is particularly useful.

Beethoven: *Werke*, edited by the Beethoven-Archiv, Bonn, published by Henle. Still in progress, this series will supersede the collected edition produced in the nineteenth century. There are several other good editions of selections of Beethoven's music, notably B. A. Wallner's edition of thirty-two piano sonatas (Munich: Henle, 1953).

Schubert: *Neue Ausgabe sämtlicher Werke*, edited by the Internationale Schubert-Gesellschaft, published by Bärenreiter. This, too, is still in progress and will gradually supersede the nineteenth-century collected edition. Howard Ferguson's edition of the piano sonatas (published by the Associated Board) is especially useful for including incomplete sonatas and many fragments in addition to the twelve complete sonatas.

Several works by these and other composers of the period have also appeared in modern facsimile editions that reproduce photographically either the autograph score or the first edition. It is quite instructive (and challenging) to attempt to play directly from these, but their main use is to allow you to check doubtful passages. It is also worth remembering that large numbers of works have not yet been published in facsimile, and often the only way to obtain a reproduction of an autograph (if one survives) or original edition is to apply to the relevant libraries. Most of this source material is held by major libraries such as The British Library, London; the Gesellschaft der Musikfreunde, Vienna; and the Staatsbibliothek zu Berlin – Preussischer Kulturbesitz.

It must be emphasized that the quality of a modern edition cannot be judged by such criteria as whether it includes fingering, or whether the editor is a well-known performer. It cannot even be judged by the length of the editorial apparatus and commentary at the beginning or end of the volume. Sometimes this material has been published separately and therefore does not appear in the volume; and it is of course impracticable to include full critical apparatus and commentary in an anthology of pieces reprinted from a variety of different modern editions. In such cases there need simply be a brief reference to where the editorial material can be found. The date of an edition can be a rough guide to its quality, since there are few good editions dating from before 1950. Also, certain publishers and editors are renowned for producing editions of high (or low!) quality. But ultimately each edition must be judged on its own merits, using the criteria and principles outlined above.

Suggestions for Further Reading

The focal point of serious musical study in the English language is *The New Grove Dictionary of Music and Musicians* (London: Macmillan – good libraries should have the second edition of 2001). The article 'Performing practice' includes a section covering the period 1750 to 1800, as well as one devoted to the nineteenth century, and its bibliography gives details of many of the original sources cited by contributors to this volume. Also useful are the articles on individual instruments, which include descriptions of how the instruments developed, many illustrations, and again detailed bibliographies. In addition to its printed format, *New Grove II* is now available to subscribers on-line: if you can get access to this version through a school, college or library, you can check subject areas such as 'Performing practice' for revisions and updates.

There is no shortage of histories of the Classical period. Two useful introductory surveys are Reinhard G. Pauly's *Music in the Classic Period*, 4th edn (Englewood Cliffs, NJ: Prentice-Hall, 2000), and Julian Rushton's well illustrated *Classical Music: A Concise History from Gluck to Beethoven* (London: Thames and Hudson, 1986). More detailed are Philip G. Downs's *Classical Music: The Era of Haydn, Mozart and Beethoven* (New York and London: W. W. Norton, 1992), and two volumes of The New Oxford History of Music, *VII: The Age of Enlightenment 1745–1790* and *VIII: The Age of Beethoven 1790–1830* (Oxford University Press, 1973 and 1982). *The Classical Era: From the 1740s to the end of the Eighteenth Century*, edited by Neal Zaslaw (London: Macmillan, 1989), contains chapters on particular musical centres in particular periods; *Haydn, Mozart and the Viennese School, 1740–80* by Daniel Heartz (New York: W. W. Norton, 1995) focuses on the most important of those centres. There is much illuminating discussion in Charles Rosen's *The Classical Style: Haydn, Mozart, Beethoven*, enlarged 3rd edn (New York: W. W. Norton; London: Faber and Faber, 1998), and Leonard G. Ratner's *Classic Music: Expression, Form and Style* (New York: Schirmer Books, 1980).

A general study of performing is *Musical Performance: A Guide to Understanding*, edited by John Rink (Cambridge University Press, 2002). Two useful introductions to historically informed interpretation are the New Grove Handbook *Performance Practice: Music after 1600*, edited by Howard Mayer Brown and Stanley Sadie (London: Macmillan, 1989), and *The Historical Performance of Music: An Introduction*, edited by Colin Lawson and Robin Stowell (Cambridge University Press, 1999).

A great deal of information about the interpretation of Classical notation is contained in Clive Brown's *Classical and Romantic Performing Practice 1750–1900* (Oxford: Clarendon Press, 1999). Important aspects of performing practice are covered in detail in Richard Hudson's *Stolen Time: The History of Tempo Rubato* (Oxford: Clarendon Press, 1996), and George Houle's *Meter in Music 1600–1800: Performance, Perception and Notation* (Bloomington, IN: Indiana University Press, 1987). How the available evidence may be applied to specific works (up to early Beethoven) is the subject of Peter le Huray's *Authenticity in Performance: Eighteenth-Century Case Studies* (Cambridge University Press, 1990).

Important original sources which have appeared in modern English translations include J. J. Quantz's *On Playing the Flute*, translated by Edward R. Reilly, 2nd edn reissue (London: Faber and Faber, 2001); C. P. E. Bach's *Essay on the True Art of Playing Keyboard Instruments*, translated by William J. Mitchell (London: Eulenburg, 1974); D. G. Türk's *School of Clavier Playing*, translated by Raymond H. Haagh (Lincoln, NE: University of Nebraska Press, 1982); J. N. Hummel's *A Complete Theoretical and Practical Course of Instructions on the Art of Playing the Piano-Forte*, Part 3, reprinted from the English translation of 1829 (London: Royal College of Music, 1992); and Leopold Mozart's *A Treatise on the Fundamental Principles of Violin Playing*, translated by Editha Knocker, 2nd edn (Oxford University Press, 1985). Despite their apparently specialist titles, all five of these contain much useful advice for all performers.

The Historical Performance of Music: An Introduction, mentioned above, is the introductory volume in a series of more specialist Cambridge Handbooks, all subtitled 'A Practical Guide'. Volumes which have appeared so far are *Early Keyboard Instruments* by David Rowland (2001), *The Early Violin and Viola* by Robin Stowell (2001), *The Early Clarinet* by our contributor Colin Lawson (2000), and *The Early Horn* by John Humphries (2000).

Cambridge University Press has also published a series of companions to different instruments (including the voice), more general in scope but still written largely from a historical perspective. The series includes: *The Cambridge Companion to the Piano*, edited by David Rowland (1998); *The Cambridge Companion to the Violin* and *The Cambridge Companion to the Cello*, both edited by Robin Stowell (1992 and 1999); *The Cambridge Companion to the Clarinet*, edited by Colin Lawson (1995); *The Cambridge Companion to Brass Instruments*, edited by Trevor Herbert and John Wallace (1997); and *The Cambridge Companion to Singing*, edited by John Potter (2000).

A general history of the early piano is Rosamond E. M. Harding's *The Piano-Forte: Its History Traced to the Great Exhibition of 1851*, 2nd edn (Old Woking: Gresham Books, 1978). One important aspect of piano playing is the subject of David Rowland's *A History of Pianoforte Pedalling* (Cambridge University Press, 1993). The instruments and repertoire of the Classical period are discussed in Richard Maunder's *Keyboard Instruments in Eighteenth-Century Vienna* (Oxford: Clarendon Press, 1998), and Katalin Komlós's *Fortepianos and their Music: Germany, America and England, 1760–1800* (Oxford: Clarendon Press, 1995). Books more specifically on keyboard interpretation include Sandra P. Rosenblum's *Performance Practices in Classic Piano Music: Their Principles and Application* (Bloomington, IN: Indiana University Press, 1988), and Bernard Harrison's *Haydn's Keyboard Music: Studies in Performance Practice* (Oxford: Clarendon Press, 1997).

Violinists, and other string players, will find much of value in Robin Stowell's *Violin Technique and Performance Practice in the Late Eighteenth and Early Nineteenth Centuries* (Cambridge University Press, 1990); Robin Stowell is also the chief contributor to *The Violin Book*, edited by Richard Dawes (London: Balafon/Outline Press, 1999). Other string instruments are covered in: Maurice W. Riley's two-volume *The History of the Viola* (Ann Arbor: Braun-Brumfield, Vol. 1, 2nd edn, 1993; Vol. 2, 1991); *One Hundred Years of Violoncello: A History of Technique and Performance Practice, 1740–1840* by Valerie Walden (Cambridge University Press, 1998); Roslyn Rensch's *The Harp: Its History, Technique and Repertoire* (London: Duckworth, 1969); and Harvey Turnbull's *The Guitar from the Renaissance to the Present Day* (London: Batsford, 1974).

There are two complementary general histories of wind instruments by Anthony Baines: *Woodwind Instruments and their History* (New York: Dover Publications, 1991), and *Brass Instruments: Their History and Development* (New York: Dover Publications, 1993). For players who do not (yet) have their own Cambridge Companions, recommended books are Nancy Toff's *The Flute Book: A Complete Guide for Students and Performers*, 2nd edn (Oxford University Press, 1997), and Günther Joppig's *The Oboe and Bassoon*, translated by Alfred Clayton (London: Batsford, 1988).

Singers do have their Cambridge Companion, and may also learn a good deal from treatises of the period such as Giovanni Battista Mancini's *Pensieri, e riflessioni pratiche sopra il canto figurato*, translated as *Practical Reflections on the Figurative Art of Singing* (Champaign, IL: Pro Musica, 1967), and *Domenico Corri's A Select Collection of the Most Admired Songs, Duetts etc., Vol. 4, and The Singer's Preceptor, Vols 1–2*, edited by Richard Maunder (New York: Garland Publishing, 1995). Vocal interpretation is discussed from a modern perspective in A. Peter Brown's *Performing Haydn's 'The Creation': Reconstructing the Earliest Renditions* (Bloomington, IN: Indiana University Press, 1986).

A clear introduction to the process of music editing is John Caldwell's *Editing Early Music*, 2nd edn (Oxford: Clarendon Press, 1995). Much more detailed is James Grier's *The Critical Editing of Music: History, Method, and Practice* (Cambridge University Press, 1996). There is a good selection of facsimiles of composers' manuscripts in *Musical Autographs from Monteverdi to Hindemith*, edited by Emanuel Winternitz (Princeton University Press, 1955; New York: Dover Publications, 1965).

Not all the books listed above are still in print; libraries may have some of them, and may be able to obtain others or suggest alternatives. Don't forget, too, that there is a great deal of information to be obtained from prefaces to editions, notes in CD booklets, magazine articles, and Internet websites. But (especially in the case of the Internet) you should always exercise your own judgement about what information is reliable and useful to you – just as you no doubt have done in reading this book.

Notes on the CD

 04.46

Haydn: Symphony No. 102 in B flat major, Finale, Presto

Royal Philharmonic Orchestra, conductor Jane Glover

From Tring Royal Philharmonic Collection TRP 042, containing the Symphonies Nos. 102 and 104

This is the witty finale of one of Haydn's last symphonies, written in London in 1794. Jane Glover, the author of our Introduction, demonstrates how the lightness and grace of the Classical style can be achieved with a relatively large orchestra of modern instruments.

 03.24

Rossini: *Semiramide*, Overture, opening

London Classical Players, conductor Roger Norrington

From Virgin Classics VM 561900-2, a collection of Rossini overtures (licensed courtesy of EMI Marketing)

For comparison, here is the sound of an orchestra of instruments of the Classical period, in the overture to Rossini's 1823 serious opera *Semiramide*. Notice the distinctive sonorities of the woodwind, the timpani, and especially the horns, with hand-stopping of notes outside the harmonic series.

 03.04

Mozart: *Le nozze di Figaro* (The Marriage of Figaro), Act II, cavatina 'Porgi amor'

Hillevi Martinpelto (soprano), English Baroque Soloists, conductor Sir John Eliot Gardiner

From Archiv 439 871-2, a three-disc set of the complete opera

At the start of Act II of Mozart's great opera of 1786, the Countess Almaviva begs the god of love to give relief to her sorrow and bring her back her errant husband, or in mercy to let her die. See Ex. 1.1 on pp. 6–7 for a voice-and-keyboard reduction of this aria, and pp. 5–9 for a detailed discussion of how it exemplifies the Classical style. Notice also the colours of the period clarinets and bassoons.

 07.49

Beethoven: Sonata in C major Op. 2 No. 3, first movement, Allegro con brio (omitting exposition repeat)

Alfred Brendel (piano)

From Philips 442 124-2, containing all three of Beethoven's Op. 2 sonatas

See David Wyn Jones's account on pp. 9–10 of Classical sonata form, with special reference to this movement from one of Beethoven's earliest piano sonatas, published in 1796. This recording (from which the repeat of the opening section has been omitted) is by a pianist widely acclaimed for his performances of music of the Classical period. Compare his modern grand piano with the historic instruments on the following tracks, including several fortepianos – a term used, incidentally, simply to distinguish the pianos of the Classical period from their modern counterparts.

 04.28

Mozart: Piano Concerto No. 23 in A major K. 488, second movement, Adagio, opening

Robert Levin (fortepiano), Academy of Ancient Music, conductor Christopher Hogwood

From L'Oiseau-Lyre 452 052-2, containing the Concertos Nos. 22 and 23

This is the start of the slow movement, in siciliana time and in the unusual key of F sharp minor, of a concerto which Mozart completed and performed in Vienna in 1786. Robert Levin, playing a copy of a fortepiano made by Anton Walter in Vienna around 1795, improvises ornamentation to fill out some of the more skeletal passages in Mozart's solo part. See p. 29 for Cliff Eisen's discussion of this practice, and a similarly ornamented passage written out by Mozart himself.

02.56

C. P. E. Bach: Fantasia in F major H. 279 (Wq. 59/5), opening

Inger Grudin-Brandt (clavichord)

From BIS-CD-142 (BIS Records, Sweden), containing keyboard music by C. P. E. and J. S. Bach played on the clavichord and fortepiano

This is the opening of a fantasia from 1782 by Carl Philipp Emanuel Bach, the second son of J. S. Bach and one of the most influential composers of the mid-eighteenth century. The intimate clavichord, with its capacity for vibrato, is well suited to C. P. E. Bach's 'expressive style'. This instrument is a copy of a clavichord made by Christian Gottlob Hubert in 1763, tuned in unequal temperament. See David Ward on pp. 40–41.

03.08

Haydn: Sonata in D major Hob. XVI/24, second movement, Adagio

Alan Curtis (harpsichord)

From Stradivarius STR 33521, volume I of a complete series of Haydn's keyboard sonatas, played on harpsichord, clavichord and fortepiano

Although we tend to think of the harpsichord as having been replaced by the piano during the later eighteenth century, many harpsichords continued to be made and played, and works such as Haydn's early keyboard sonatas were written with the harpsichord primarily in mind. This slow movement of a Haydn sonata first published in 1774 (its inconclusive ending is explained by the fact that it leads straight into the finale) is played on a copy of a 1769 harpsichord by the French instrument maker Pascal Taskin. See David Ward on p. 40.

06.25

Mozart: Sonata in C major K. 330, second movement, Andante cantabile

David Ward (fortepiano)

From Meridian CDE 84239, containing the whole of K. 330 and other keyboard works by Mozart

Our contributor David Ward plays this Mozart slow movement, from a sonata of the early 1780s, on a copy of a fortepiano by Anton Walter, a Viennese maker whose instruments Mozart knew and admired. See p. 44 for a picture of a Walter instrument which Mozart owned. Notice the varied decoration applied to the repeats of this movement: for more on Classical ornamentation see pp. 28–34.

03.20

Clementi: Sonata in F major Op. 33 No. 2, third movement, Presto

Andreas Staier (fortepiano)

From Teldec 3984-26731-2, a recital of sonatas and other keyboard works by Clementi (℗ 2000 Teldec Classics International GmbH. Used by permission of Warner Classics, Warner Music UK and Warner Strategic Marketing.)

This is the finale of a sonata published in 1794 by Muzio Clementi, who was born in Italy but lived mostly in England from 1785 until his death in 1832. It is played on a fortepiano made by John Broadwood & Son in about 1802, an example of the English type of piano which David Ward describes on p. 43.

02.47

Schubert: Moment musical in A flat major D. 780 No. 2, opening

Olga Tverskaya (fortepiano)

From Opus 111 OPS-30-139, containing the six *Moments musicaux* together with Schubert's late A major Sonata D. 959

This is the start of a Schubert piano piece from the 1820s, played on a piano of about 1820 by the Viennese maker Conrad Graf (see p. 44). In a note for her recording, Olga Tverskaya describes how the instrument 'brings out the warm, singing sound that is so intrinsic to Schubert', and how, 'whereas in performance on a modern instrument one tends to make greater use of the dynamic range available, the fortepianist is able to take advantage of the tone colours and contrasts between the registers to their full extent'.

03.29

Beethoven: Sonata for cello and piano in A major Op. 69, third movement, Adagio cantabile introduction and first section of Allegro vivace

David Watkin (cello), Howard Moody (fortepiano)

From Chandos Chaconne CHAN 0561, containing three of Beethoven's sonatas for cello and piano

This is the opening of Beethoven's A major Sonata of 1807–8, originally described (as were all Beethoven's cello works) as for keyboard and cello. The fortepiano in this recording is another Graf, dating from 1826 and similar to one that Graf made for Beethoven a few years before the composer's death; the cello is a 1709 instrument, set up as it would have been in the early nineteenth century. The cello playing exemplifies many of the points made by Duncan Druce in Chapter 4 'Strings'.

03.01

Mozart: String Quartet in D minor K. 421, third movement, Menuetto (Allegretto) and Trio, as far as the end of the Trio

Quatuor Mosaïques

From Auvidis Astrée E 8746, volume I of a series of the six quartets dedicated to Haydn, containing the Quartet in G major K. 387, and this D minor Quartet

Classical string style in ensemble music is demonstrated in this recording of the minuet and trio (without the reprise of the minuet) of Mozart's D minor Quartet of 1783. Notice how the crisp bow-strokes and the sparing vibrato of this celebrated period-instrument quartet give the music a lighter texture than when it is played on modern instruments.

03.54

Mozart: Concerto for flute and harp in C major K. 299, second movement, Andantino, opening

Lisa Beznosiuk (flute), Frances Kelly (harp), Academy of Ancient Music, director Christopher Hogwood

From L'Oiseau Lyre 417 622-2, a disc of Mozart's wind concertos, including also the Flute Concerto in G major and the Bassoon Concerto

This recording of part of Mozart's double concerto of 1778 demonstrates the sonorities and articulation both of the harp of the Classical period (see p. 63) and of the Classical flute (see p. 67). The orchestra is directed from the keyboard, a Baroque practice that continued in some places well into the Classical era.

03.58

Mozart: Serenade in C minor K. 388, second movement, Andante

The English Concert Winds

From Hyperion CDA 66887, containing this serenade, the Serenade in E flat major K. 375, and contemporary wind arrangements of three Mozart overtures

Mozart's C minor Serenade of 1782 or '83 is written for an ensemble of pairs of oboes, clarinets, horns and bassoons, slightly smaller than the group depicted on p. 66. In this recording, notice, as well as the sonorities and blend of the period instruments, the decoration introduced by the first clarinettist (our contributor Colin Lawson) in the reprise.

04.31

Weber: Clarinet Concerto No. 1 in F minor, first movement, Allegro, opening

Colin Lawson (clarinet), The Hanover Band, conductor Roy Goodman

From Classic FM 75605 57019 2, containing the two Concertos and Concertino by Weber and the First Concerto by Spohr

Although Weber's short life fell entirely within the Classical period as we have defined it for this volume, his music looks forward to the Romantic era – as in the drama of the opening tutti of this concerto of 1811, and the operatic expressiveness of some of the solo writing. The solo part is played by Colin Lawson on a copy of a ten-keyed boxwood clarinet made by Heinrich Grenser in about 1810.

02.44

Mozart: *Le nozze di Figaro*, opening recitative of Act III

Rodney Gilfry (baritone), Hillevi Martinpelto (soprano), Alison Hagley (soprano), Sabine Vatin (fortepiano), Timothy Mason (cello), English Baroque Soloists, conductor Sir John Eliot Gardiner

From Archiv 439 871-2, as in Track above

Act III of Mozart's *Le nozze di Figaro* begins with a passage of *recitativo secco*, i.e. accompanied only by keyboard and (here) cello. At first Count Almaviva is alone, reflecting on the odd goings-on in the previous act; the Countess and her maid Susanna enter in the background, conspiring to trap the Count into an assignation which will reveal his philandering; then Susanna comes forward to set the plot in motion. In this recording, notice the conversational quality of the singing, and also the insertion of appoggiaturas, discussed by Richard Wigmore on pp. 81–3.

03.53

Gluck: *Orfeo ed Euridice*, aria 'Che farò senza Euridice?'

Derek Lee Ragin (alto), English Baroque Soloists, conductor Sir John Eliot Gardiner

From Philips 434 093-2, a two-disc set of the complete opera in its original version, first performed in Vienna in 1762

This famous aria is sung by Orpheus when he has recovered his wife Eurydice from the land of the dead but then, through his own impatience, lost her again for ever: 'What shall I do without Eurydice?... There is no hope for me, neither on earth nor in heaven'. On this recording, the aria (originally written for a castrato mezzo-soprano) is sung with Domenico Corri's ornamentation of the final return of the melody, illustrated on p. 84.

03.42

Mozart: 'Non sò d'onde viene', concert aria, K. 294, first section of main aria

Natalie Dessay (soprano), Orchestre de l'Opéra de Lyons, conductor Theodor Guschlbauer

From EMI CDC 5 55386 2, a collection of Mozart concert arias

Mozart wrote this aria in 1778, on an existing operatic text, as a showpiece for the soprano Aloysia Weber. After the opening recitative, the text describes the character's conflicting feelings of tenderness and coldness. This recording incorporates the decorations by Mozart himself illustrated on p. 85.

 03.44

Schubert: *Winterreise*, sixth song, 'Wasserflut' (Flood)

Max van Egmond (baritone), Jos van Immerseel (fortepiano)

From Channel Classics CCS 0190, a recording of the complete cycle

This song from Schubert's 1827 cycle *Winterreise* (Winter Journey) describes the traveller's tears falling in the snow; when the snow melts, the stream of tears will lead to the house of his beloved. The recording uses a copy of a Walter fortepiano, which the performers consider more suitable than later Viennese instruments for 'this most intimate of song cycles'. The same feeling is reflected in the singer's unforced, room-scale approach. The later stanzas are lightly ornamented, as described on p. 88. Notice incidentally the careful separation throughout of dotted rhythms and triplets – one possible solution to the 'vexed question' raised by Cliff Eisen on pp. 24–5.